The Psychic Power
of Running

The
PSYCHIC
POWER
of RUNNING

*How the Body
Can Illuminate
the Mysteries of the Mind*

by Valerie Andrews

Rawson, Wade Publishers, Inc./New York

To my parents

The author gratefully acknowledges permission to quote from the following:

ANTI-DEPRESSANT RUNNING by John H. Greist, copyright 1978 by John H. Greist, The Madison Running Press, Madison, Wis.

RUN TO REALITY by John H. Greist and Roger Eischens, copyright 1975 by John H. Greist and Roger Eischens, The Madison Running Press, Madison, Wis.

THE JOY OF RUNNING by Thaddeus Kostrubala, copyright 1976 by Thaddeus Kostrubala, J. B. Lippincott Co., Philadelphia, Pa.

GETTING WELL AGAIN by Carl O. Simonton, Stephanie Matthews-Simonton, and James Creighton, copyright 1978 by Carl O. Simonton, Stephanie Matthews-Simonton, and James Creighton, J. P. Tarcher, Inc., Los Angeles, Calif.

NEW AGE COACH by Dyveke Spino, from an unpublished manuscript copyright 1976 by Dyveke Spino.

BEYOND JOGGING by Michael Spino, copyright 1976 by Michael Spino, Celestial Arts, Millbrae, Calif.

RUNNING HOME by Michael Spino, copyright 1977 by Michael Spino, Celestial Arts, Millbrae, Calif.

Library of Congress Cataloging in Publication Data

Andrews, Valerie.
    The psychic power of running.

    Bibliography: p.
    Includes index.
    1. Jogging—Psychological aspects.   2. Running—Psychological aspects.   I.   Title.
GV494.A5   1978   128′.2   77–92075
ISBN 0–89256–057–6

Acknowledgments

I would like to express my appreciation to the New York Academy of Sciences for making available the most recent findings on the medical and psychological effects of long-distance running, and also to thank the following individuals: Dr. Marlin Mackenzie, of Columbia University for sharing his case histories on women runners; Dr. David Shainberg and Lawrence Shainberg, for their observations on distance running as a form of meditation; Dr. Thomas Bassler, for information on runners' diets, the aging process, and immunity to atherosclerotic forms of coronary heart disease; Michael Murphy, Mike Spino, George Leonard, and Steven Donovan, at Esalen, for their ongoing study of running as a touchstone to altered states of consciousness; Dr. Thaddeus Kostrubala, of San Diego, for the concept of Paleoanalytic Psychology—the biological and psychological aspects of man's evolution as a runner and hunter—gatherer; Teresa Clitsome and Austin Gontang, running therapists from the San Diego Marathon Clinic; Dr. John Greist and Roger Eischens, of the University of Wisconsin, for case studies of depression and the running cure; Dr. William Glasser for his views on jogging as a positive addiction and means of combating drug abuse and alcoholism; Professor Julian Jaynes, of Princeton University, for his thoughts on visceral perceptions of early man; Dr. Joyce Goodrich and Dr. Lawrence LeShan, for their research on meditation as an aid to psychic healing; Dr. Carl Simonton, for his study of the combined effects of guided imagery and running on the body's immune system; Inventor Itzhak Bentov, for his lucid explanation of the biophysics of altered states of consciousness; Nina Kuscsik and Kathrine Switzr, for their personal accounts of the rise of women's running;

v

Carol Dilfer, for her ideas on exercise during pregnancy; Fred Lebow and Paul Fetscher, of New York Roadrunner's Club; Joe Henderson, of *Runner's World* magazine, and Walt Stack, of the San Francisco Dolphin South End Club, my guides to West Coast running; to researcher Orel Protopopescu, and two stalwarts of organization, typists Natalie Parnass and Larry Paulette.

I would also like to thank my agent, Harvey Klinger, and Kennett and Eleanor Rawson, for their editorial vision and support; Katheryn Lance, a frequent running companion and authority in women's fitness; my friends, Sally van Wagenen Keil and Robert Karen; and Thomas McKnight, the touchstone for many theories of body-mind transformation.

VALERIE ANDREWS
New York, February, 1978

Contents

Acknowledgments   v

1. Inner-Directed Running: Jogging for Personal Growth
   and Self-Expansion   3

2. Rediscovering the Body: How Running Re-awakens
   Body Feelings   8
   • The Basic Synchronicity of Body-Mind   11
   • Running As Body Therapy   14
   • How to Get Started: Some Practical Advice   26

3. Running Away from Depression   33
   • The Biochemical Basis for Behavior   33
   • Chasing Away the Sedentary Blues   35
   • Anger and Hostility: Draining off Negative
     Emotions in the Run   41

4. Anxiety and Fear: Running to Control Your "Fight
   or Flight" Response   44
   • Anxiety and Breathlessness   45
   • Learning to Trust Your Body   47
   • How to Use Running to Confront Your Irrational
     Fears   49

5. The Runner's High: Replacement for Negative
   Addictions   51
   • Getting Strong: Running Away from Self-
     Destructive Thoughts   52
   • Learning to Give Yourself Pleasure   55
   • Advice to the Injured Runner   57

6. Running Reborn: Jogging and Life-Style
   Change   59

- Rediscovering Your Biorhythmic Cycles   59
- Running Away from Heart Disease: The Number One Killer Is Your Sedentary Life-Style   61
- The Prevention Diet: Bringing the Body Back to Normal   65
- Run Longer—Live Longer   66
- Jogging and Personality Change   68

7. How Running Unravels the Mysteries of the Unconscious   78
  - A New Model of the Psyche   78
  - Resonating with Your Unconscious in the Run   81
  - Dreams and Visions   83
  - The Runner's Journal: The Key to Interpreting the Mysteries of the Unconscious Mind   88
  - Decoding the Messages from the Dark Side of the Psyche   92

8. How to Meditate in Motion: Running As the Western Zen   96
  - The Physiology of Meditation: The Biological Process of the Run   100
  - End-Watching vs. Beginner's Mind   103
  - How to Reach the Meditative State   106
  - The Way of the Body: Running and Sensory Awareness Meditation   107

9. Spiritual Athletes: The New Elite   111
  - The Simultaneous Transformation of the Body and the Mind   112
  - The Esalen Training Program: A Variety of Tempos and Gaits   114
  - The Esalen Meditation and Mental Imagery Program   119

, 10. The Road to Health: How Running Fosters Psychic Healing   123
- Increasing Your Receptivity to Healing Thoughts   123
- Running and Meditation: Radical Adjunct Cancer Therapy   124
- A General Healing Meditation   125
- Healing Ourselves As We Heal Others   128
- Healing Methods in a Running Culture   130

11. Runner's Cosmology: From the Physical to the Metaphysical in a Moving Universe   133
- A Return to the World View of the Greeks   133
- Modern Cosmology and the Mystical Mind-Space of the Run   135
- Movement and the Collective Mind   138

12. Creativity and Success: How Running Builds Self-Confidence and Brain Power   141
- Building a Model for Success   144
- Building a Success Image   147
- Increasing Your Brain Power   150
- Running As an Antidote to Overthink   154
- Running As an Antidote to Overwork   155

13. Toward a New Androgyny: How Running Makes Women More Independent and Assertive   158
- When Women's Running Took Wings   159
- Running Through Psychological Barriers: Fears and Peer-Group Pressures   161
- "Why Can't a Woman Be More Like a Man?"   164
- How This New Self-Assertiveness Spills Over into Social Life   169

- Pregnancy: How Running Conquers Fears of Helplessness and Dependency 173
- Getting Started after Forty 176

14. The Primal Run 179
- Visceral Learning 180
- A Return to the Values of the Run 185

Bibliography 191

Index 197

*The Psychic Power
of Running*

ONE

Inner-Directed Running: Jogging for Personal Growth and Self-Expansion

---

As we stand on the threshold of a cultural reawakening to the psychological restorative values of sport, running—the least self-conscious and most natural of our movements—has made the wisdom of the body accessible to virtually everyone, regardless of age or athletic ability.

Over 25 million people who started jogging as the fastest, most convenient way to get in shape are suddenly finding their daily workouts can trigger far-reaching changes in the body and the mind. Now, through a blend of self-awareness exercises and a regular running program, we can gain greater insights into our behavior, drain off tensions and negative emotions, heighten creativity, and enter altered states of consciousness. Jogging has become the tool for transformation in a new, holistic age.

The search for self-actualization through sport goes back, in Western civilization, to the sacred games of the Greeks in the seventh century B.C.—when men learned to transcend the dynamics of fate through heroic action in the dust and clamor of the Olympic arena. In our own time, we have had to wrench our Achilles' heels from the viselike grip of an industrial age—in which man's physical being became as regimented and predictable as the machine—

and slowly rediscover the ways to find meaning in life through physical movement.

In the 1960s, a handful of initiates began turning to the Eastern disciplines—aikido, karate, and T'ai Chi—not only for the grace and economy of movement but for the attendant philosophies of mind. Then, the majority of weekend athletes began to experience the inner dimensions of sport, as Timothy Gallwey gave us "inner games"—a combination of Zen and modern psychology that enabled us to go beyond the rigid reconstruction of technique and defeat those inner fears that hampered our performance on the ski slopes and the tennis courts. Finally, the running revolution has enabled everyone to achieve the level of fitness that guarantees the unity and well-being of body and soul, without gamesmanship, rules, and special equipment—and in the shortest possible time.

The aim of this book is to show you how to foster profound alterations in life-style and consciousness with inner-directed running. Inner-directed means tuning in to the psychological process unfolding in the run and tuning out external goals and thoughts of competition. Paradoxically, as you run in the service of personal growth, you will unleash hidden energies—psychic and physical—that will enable you to run faster and farther than you ever did before.

The secret of inner-directed running is in the power of the body to illuminate the mysteries of the mind. In the first few weeks of training, we establish a cleaner body and a clearer mind by burning off the biochemical wastes that are also the carriers of negative emotions. Then, we begin to liberate the myriad emotions that are "stuck" inside our bodies. Whenever we are angry or afraid, we clamp down on different parts of the body, accumulating muscular "knots." As we run, the increased oxygen flow and circulation of the body literally breaks down these dead spots and soon we start to rediscover body feelings of which we were only dimly aware before.

In the next stage of our training, we learn to stave off unpleasant shifts in mood and stem those feelings of powerlessness that suffocate a healthy zest for life. We can even rid ourselves of specific fears and anxieties since jogging enables us to control the physical symptoms of anxiety—a pounding of the heart and breathlessness—and helps us handle our biological "fight or flight" reaction in threatening situations.

After we've gone through these initial stages of purification, we almost unconsciously begin to make major alterations in our life-style. Because we have more energy, we find we're working harder and possibly thinking of a career switch to make better use of our new vitality. We find we've lost our fascination with the passive acquisition of material possessions and instead now prefer involvement with relationships and want to become active consumers of travel and adventure to satisfy our greater longing for *experience*. By now, we've also resumed our natural cycles of eating, sleeping, and mating—we have become attuned to the seasons of the body and stopped adhering to the arbitrary strictures of routine. Suddenly we find that running has become the major organizing element of our lives!

Just as jogging fosters changes in the outer life, it also acts as the catalyst for internal change, strengthening and reorganizing the personality and activating the deepest drives of the unconscious. At this level, we learn to integrate the well of imagery and psychic information that springs spontaneously from the run with messages we receive in dreams. Joggers dream more vividly and more often than their sedentary counterparts and also develop a personal mythology to interpret the spiritual and religious rebirth that is kindled by the run.

Running also brings us to a transcendental state much faster than does sitting meditation. And through the use of "guided imagery" and meditations on the wholeness of the body we can activate the body's natural immune system and facilitate psychic healing in the run.

Then, too, as we begin to approach our optimum level of fitness, we may experience startling transformations of the body and the mind, with major advances in both athletic capabilities and consciousness occurring all at once. When you run your first six miles at a five-minute pace, you may have simultaneous breakthroughs into altered states of awareness, ranging from the experience of "cosmic consciousness," to heightened powers of telepathy, clairvoyance, and even out-of-body states.

The cultivation of the body as the touchstone to greater psychic powers goes back to the ancient Greek and Egyptian mystery schools, where physical exercises for opening the lotus of the mind were passed on secretly from one master to the next and practiced in strictest isolation. Today we are experiencing the great transformation of consciousness in groups. As you undoubtedly know, whenever we run together we reach a much higher energy level, enabling us to run farther and faster than we ever could alone. While it is desirable to run by yourself for the purpose of introspection and to gain deeper insights into your personal life, you achieve something quite different when you run with other people, a "synchronous bonding" that allows you to delve deeper into meditative states.

If all of this sounds mystical, remember that the greatest mystics can be the most efficient human beings, for they can put their increased energies to work on the most practical levels. Heightened powers of concentration developed in the run can also aid us in our creative efforts. We can increase our productivity and problem-solving abilities by performing certain mental exercises as we jog. And we can also make our regular training program a model for success that spills over into our professional lives by setting up a basic system of incentive and maintenance goals. In addition, jogging washes away the accumulated body tensions of a day's work and provides an antidote to mental strain.

Women can become more independent, self-confident, and assertive through a psychologically oriented program of distance training. Surprisingly, the gap between the sexes narrows with the distance—for the longer we run, the more likely it is the women can outlast and even outrun the men. Moreover, when women reach this state of physical development, they achieve a balance of masculine and feminine personality traits. This androgyny of body, mind, and spirit is reflected in feelings of self-mastery and physical control, freedom from self-criticism and fear of social approbation, and a healthy love of competition, new forms of "feminine power" liberated in the run.

The ability to run long distances is the one genetic characteristic that made man more durable to begin with. It was a rotating femur and full upright stance that enabled early man to move fluidly and freely over the grassy savannahs of his birth and to outdistance his imperfectly postured ancestors, the lumbering forest apes. Now we must wonder if the present mass recognition of our biological need to run isn't an instinctive drive to recapitulate our primary genetic strengths before the next evolutionary leap into the future. For in the crucible of the run we can experience all the transformations of which man is capable and embark upon a fantastic journey through the pathways of the senses, leading to the furthest reaches of the mind.

TWO

Rediscovering the Body: How Running Re-awakens Body Feelings

"Most of the time I live my life half in and half out. I have always felt I couldn't depend on myself and I really couldn't do anything. When things get too scary I fade out. But in running I cannot fade out. For the first time in my life I've discovered I can do it—I can be here, as I run three miles one day, five miles the next . . ."

How many of us have momentarily lost our place in the world because we've neglected to establish a firm foundation in the body? Feelings of anxiety and anomie are often the result of our alienation from the body and its natural rhythms. Like the man who "fades out" when things get too scary, we lost the sense of who we are physically *and* emotionally. "We" simply do not exist because we do not feel the viscous fibers of our muscles holding us together.

When we are not grounded in the sensations of the body we bear the brunt of our physical insecurity in marred personal relationships. According to psychiatrist Frederick Baekeland, active adults who suddenly stop exercising report an increased desire for praise and reassurance and a greater need to be with other people. In short, they become dependent on others to give them what their bodies normally do: a sense of pride in their efforts and a feeling of self-worth and belonging.

Sticking to a regular running program is the quickest and most convenient way to build independence and self-confidence while you improve your physical condition. "Before I started running, I'd come home after a bad day of trading and expect to be fussed over," explained John H, a forty-year-old bond broker on Wall Street. "I needed constant attention and approval from my family, and if I didn't get it I'd sulk. Now, regardless of any minor setbacks, I feel I've accomplished one sure thing every afternoon wtih my five-mile after-work jog through Central Park."

Rosalie P, a divorcée in her early thirties, found running made her more self-assured and less dependent on men. "Just getting out and running a few miles a week showed me what I could do to improve my mood and outlook on life. I no longer need a boyfriend to make me feel I'm 'somebody.' And men actually respond better to me because they feel less threatened. They know I have something else in my life that makes me a full and vibrant human being."

Physical activity also promotes a clarity of mind, and running enables us to unify our thoughts and actions. Our mental processes become geared to our physical ones when we jog. Hence there is less likelihood of "fading out," or feeling no connection with other people or things. Moreover, if your thinking is disorganized or dissociated, and you go out for a run, suddenly you'll find a natural narrative forming as you regulate your heartbeat and your breath. One banker from Chicago gets up from his desk when his thoughts begin to come too fast and furiously for him to make any sense out of them at all. "After a mile or two, my body and mind have come together and I'm thinking at a much more manageable rate."

Plato knew that thoughts not connected to the body would be emotionally unsettling and counterproductive. He advised, in the *Timaeus,* to avoid exercising body or mind without the other in order to preserve an equal and healthy balance between them:

> Anyone engaged in mathematics or any other strenuous intellectual pursuit should also exercise his body and take part in physical training. By such moderate action he can reduce to order and system, the qualities and constituents that wander through the body.

The more time we spend on intellectual pursuits, the more physical exercise we need to wash away the mental tensions and to reestablish a basic harmony between the body and the mind. Today over 25 million joggers are instinctively compensating for their high-stress but sedentary desk jobs with their daily runs. The New York Academy of Sciences has even found a correlation between intense intellectual activity and the number of miles put in: it seems that those who think the hardest and continually perform under pressure run the farthest. Over 96 percent of the "elite class" distance runners—sub-three-hour marathoners who train as heavily as 300 miles a month—are professionals with college training in education, business administration, science, and the law.

Those of us who are over-educated and under-exercised are generally compulsive personalities—we cling to a battery of preconceived notions about how we should think, act, and feel. We're no longer amenable to change and lose our spontaneity. We make lists and devise elaborate systems of delayed gratification so we can continue plowing through our work. But running restores us to a state of nature, and the sensations of the body bring us into the "here and now." We enter a world of innocence and leave behind our arrogant belief that everything should be quantified and known.

The Basic Synchronicity of Body-Mind

"I usually try to make everything fit my plans," explains a Manhattan psychiatrist, "but I never run according to a plan I have arranged or information I've accumulated about the perfect run. I learn by watching what happens every moment. The whole of the run—the body-brain-time-space event—is an irreversible biological process in action. It is not something that I 'do' but happens according to a movement of its own."

We all were born with a basic synchronicity of body and mind, but those of us who think a lot tend to forget how our emotions and body feelings are intertwined. Psychoanalyst Wilhelm Reich believed that undischarged emotions could be "stuck" in rigid or clamped-down sections of the body, and that the free flow of energy throughout the system was a prerequisite for mental health.

Early emotional insecurities trigger a full-fledged body response. Psychosomatic asthma usually develops when children and adolescents fear not having adequate physical control over their environment. And these young people generally use metaphors of bodily disintegration and dispersal to describe their feelings before and during the attack.

Of course, the reverse is also true. Children rushed too rapidly through the crawling and creeping stage of motor development exhibit reduced verbal abilities and often remain ill at ease for the rest of their lives. It now seems reasonable to suggest that those deficient in the running stage of motor coordination may lack certain relational skills—such as the ability to judge relationships objectively and feel secure in their ability to master their surroundings. In fact, running serves as a natural bulwark against fears of helplessness and abandonment in children. When a Montessori school in southern California held a twenty-seven-mile fund-raising walk-jog to the ocean, one six-year-old who had completed the entire distance disarmingly told her mother, "Do you realize I could get lost anywhere—but I'd be able to jog out?"

But running also can help us as adults to reestablish a dialogue between the body and the mind. We can use our workouts as a way to tune into body cues that we might otherwise ignore as we attend to routine responsibilities.

Austin Gontang, a Gestalt therapist in San Diego, believes running expedites therapy because it brings out repressed body feelings and enables people to be more honest about their emotions. When one of his patients, Marion R, was about to be divorced, Gontang took her for a five-mile run. Suddenly Marion got a pain in her side, the first sign of unresolved tension regarding the final separation from her husband. Gontang asked her to keep on running.

After a few paces he asked, "How is it now?"

"It's in my chest," she replied, and started running faster. "Now it's in my throat . . ."

"Who has you by the throat?"

"My husband . . ."

Gontang took the lead and increased the speed. "What's happening to you? What does the pain feel like?"

"A knife . . ."

"Who has the knife?" he shouted as they accelerated around a curve.

"My husband!" She began to sob deeply as she realized her relationship with her husband had been "choking her off" and threatening the very marrow of her existence.

Though she was deeply anxious about the difficulties of the marriage and of the divorce, until she began to breathe hard in the final stages of the run, she was unable to release her tension and cry.

Usually it's hard to get people to let go and really sob in therapy, Gontang explains. But running lowers our resistance and brings us closer to our emotional core. As we breathe fully, it's impossible to stay rigid, to maintain the stiff upper lip and the sucked-in belly of the stoic pose.

"It's surprising how many people don't believe they can rely on their own bodies to sustain them in times of crisis," Gontang adds. He once jogged twelve miles with a client about to lose a job he had held for fifteen years, due to a major company cutback. This accomplished runner was unable to keep up his usual pace without stressing his breathing and his heart. He said he was terrified at the thought of telling his wife they'd have to give up the mortgage on their home as he searched for work. "We didn't talk about the firing," Gontang explains. "Instead we did nothing but work on his breathing in the run. If he could support himself physically in his distress, he would be able to support himself emotionally, too."

Frequently the body spontaneously begins to realign itself during the run and certain complexes of physical "armor" begin to be released. One young woman describes such a breakthrough on an early morning workout:

"Something in my body opened up. I started running faster and faster and I began to cry. I could feel the seams of my life separating down the middle of my body. As I kept on running, details of my childhood flashed through my mind. All the times I had told myself I was inadequate when my parents expected too much of me—all the times I had said, 'I can't,' were breaking up inside of me like mounds of glacial insecurity. I felt the anger and tensions and hurt drain away, and soon I could feel the strength of my body as I ran effortlessly—as I had as a little girl."

Running As Body Therapy

Because of the powerful range of emotions associated with body movement, many psychotherapists have found jogging a useful tool. According to Dr. Marlin Mackenzie, a therapist and researcher in sports psychology at Columbia University, anyone who understands how to express her or himself through physical activity is likely to get through therapy faster than a sedentary counterpart, simply because such a person has learned to listen to the messages of the body and to open up the emotional energy flowing through physical channels.

One of Mackenzie's patients was Jane K. A graduate of Vassar, and an editor at an academic publishing house, Jane had always thought of herself as an "intellectual" and her body as the extra baggage she must carry through life. She started jogging to shed the few pounds she had gained in five years at a desk job, and she soon began to rediscover those body feelings that she had lost or put away. Mackenzie instructed her to run the full three miles to and from his office, paying particular attention to her thoughts and body sensations. Then he asked Jane to "dialogue" with those body parts that she was most aware of in the run. From these excerpts from the initial session, you can see how running sets up a dialogue between the body and the mind and brings the self-image and body image into sharper focus.

> **Patient:** I hadn't run for a while and when I started to do four miles down here, my ankles began to stiffen up. I was also feeling especially fat in the beginning of the run. And I hated my stomach. Then I started

hating my behind and getting very hostile about my body.

Therapist: Could you take the role of the stomach and speak to yourself?

P: I was thinking "Oh, you goddamn stomach. Why do you feel so big today?" And then my stomach would say something like, "Well, I'm full of a lot of gas because you haven't been moving me enough. And I'm bloating so you'll pay attention to me. And so you'll let me move instead of making me sit still all the time." And then I'd say, "Well, you're right. But I'm running now. What more do you want?" And my stomach would say, "Well, you have to run more often because I can't stand sitting inside you all day in front of your typewriter. It's boring."

T: How do you respond to that?

P: "You're right. I don't pay enough attention to you." And then my stomach says, "That's just an excuse. You're afraid that I'm going to stay like this even if you *do* exercise."

T: Now imagine you're a third person overhearing this conversation. What would you say?

P: That the person had an irrational fear and the stomach was right.

T: What would you say to the two?

P: It would be better if you guys started doing something together instead of fighting this out all the time. But then of course, I get into another thing. I think, "Why should I pay attention to my stomach if it makes me so miserable all the time?" If I start thinking about how nice and tight and firm I want it to be, like it was when I sixteen and taking gym classes, then I have to realize what it is now. Which is definitely NOT that.

T: You wish you were back to being nice and firm when you were a girl in gym class? In your teens?

P: Yes. But I was excused from gym a lot.

T: What was the occasion for the excuses?

P: I didn't mind the activity, and in junior high school I even had some talent for the skills. But I never got along with my gym teachers and so I developed a severe hatred for it. Later on I would panic whenever I had to run, and I'd start to breathe heavily and no one ever took me aside to say, "What's causing this?" Instead, when we had to jog out to the field, which was half a mile away, and then do the six-hundred-yard run, my gym teacher accused me of deliberately slowing down and made me run the course four times. Every time I ran it, I had to stop in the middle. I was really humiliated because I couldn't conquer this running thing. And nobody was *helping* me with it. They were making it worse.

T: What kind of excuse did you use when you got out of gym?

P: Period cramps.

T: That connects to the stomachache you had today.

P: What I felt today wasn't an ache, it was a bloat. An uncomfortable fullness. Like when you think you're going to throw up and feel there's a balloon stuck in your throat. You're on the verge of being nauseous and you can't quite retch it out . . .

T: So there was some disgust associated with this stomachache?

P: Yes. It was a bloated, decadent, full . . . you know, *unelegant* feeling. Something . . . fat about it.

T: What was your body like as a teen-ager?

P: I think my weight was about the same as it is now . . .

T: Trim.

P: Yes. My *size* was the same then. But I wasn't really . . . most of my friends were *really* skinny.

T: So in comparison you were fat.

P: Yes.

T: Fat stomach, fat Janie . . .

P: I didn't have the stomach problems then. It was more my ass. If I ever went over to somebody's house and didn't bring all the clothes I'd need for the weekend, my friend would say, "Oh, here, you can wear a pair of my jeans." When you can't get them up, you just—Aaaaaah—you HATE yourself.

T: What happened to your body today?

P: My ankles tightened up after I'd been running for a while. About that point I started thinking, "God, are you SLOW today."

T: So the ankle pain came just as you were chastising yourself . . .

P: Yes. I was running at a crawl and would have given anything for an excuse to stop. Because I was having to face not doing so well. And I don't like that very much. Then I thought, "Maybe if I keep on running I'll just work it through."

T: What do you mean "work it through"?

P: Get past it. I think one of my biggest faults is that whenever anything unpleasant starts to happen, instead of letting it happen and realizing that it's not going to last forever, I resist. But my running's helping me learn that I'm not going to have that ankle pain forever. And by extension if I have an argument with somebody, that's not going to last forever. Pain always gives way to something else.

T: What happened inside you—just before it went away?

P: I started feeling lighter and faster.

T: Do you recall what you were thinking about or what you were looking at while that was going on?

P: I crossed the bridge and went down to the path by the river and felt an almost instant surge. Somehow the movement of the river was pulling me along. I wasn't running and calculating my speed against cold immovable steel buildings, or against people watching me.

T: Sounds like you got some sort of charge that you absorbed from the river. Then you let your body flow.

P: It was really a good metaphor—the river was swelling, too. Almost like a breath. So I started breathing with the river swelling.

T: When you allowed the inner part of you to be expressed and you had a metaphor to tune in to yourself, then your running went better?

P: Much better.

T: What I'd like you to do is start with the beginning of your run and reminisce about what you saw and experienced.

P: First I had too much on and I hate that because I have to start peeling off layers and tying them around my waist, like streamers.

T: Would those make you look foolish?

P: I have to keep fussing all the time—to keep from losing something. But today I didn't mind. When I first felt the warmth I thought "Hot. Spring!" and took a completely new route. So I had the feeling of anticipation, "Gee, what am I going to do today. Where am I going to go?" And as I started running, I was aware that people on the street were looking at me.

T: What people?

P: The sidewalks were crowded with people doing their marketing. And there were some young kids, a couple of thirteen-year-old boys. One said, "Hey, Mama!" as I passed.

T: How did you feel then?

P: Amused. I wanted to turn around and say, "Hey, Mama, *what?* Don't just say something like that. I don't know what you mean!"

T: Did you feel angry?

P: Yes, but angry mixed with curious. If I were *walking* down the street and somebody said that, I'd think how rude! But maybe he was being complimentary. He might have thought, "Hey, she's *running*. Good for her." So in a situation where I normally would have said, "Uh—you creep!" I wanted to say, "Well, how *are* you responding to me? What *do* you think?" After I got past them there were some little old ladies who were getting nervous because I was approaching them. They thought I was going to run them down. I was kind of cutting it pretty close until I got right up to them—then I jumped over a puddle to give them room. Maybe I was showing off.

T: You were saying "Look, ladies, look what I can do!"

P: Then there was another woman in her late fifties. Trim enough to be doing what I was doing. And she had on a little ski jacket. I wanted to see something of her face as I went by, some sort of flicker of recognition, because I thought she was an athletic type. But she had the stoniest face I'd ever seen.

T: What did you feel when you got the stone face?

P: Disappointment. Real disappointment.

T: What would you want to say to her?

P: I'd want to ask her *why* she was wearing the ski jacket. And if she ever used it. And if she didn't, *why not?*

T: Is that important?

P: Since I started running it's important to me to move as much as possible. And I think it should be important to everybody else.

T: A little bit of projection going on . . . What were you experiencing inside while you were seeing all this?

P: I was afraid that I'd start running too fast. And when I start out too fast it takes me longer to warm up. The muscles stay stiff longer. Whereas if I just gradually . . .

T: *The* muscles?

P: Yeah, all of them.

T: Say "I"—not them.

P: Oh, I always thought it was *them*.

T: No! Why dissociate from *your* muscles by saying *the* muscles? Why not say it takes *me* longer to warm up . . .

P: I guess I never thought of *them* as *me*.

T: But you think of your stomach and your ass as you. The *bad* part of you.

P: But at that point I was trying not to think about myself at all. I just wanted to let myself be. Sometimes I try not to think because my brain gets in the way.

T: That's tricky. You're working hard not to deal with yourself.

P: That's because everybody always told me I try too hard. So I'm trying *not* to. What I want to do is remove a layer. Remove that distance I feel from my body. Maybe that's what I do when I meditate while running . . . I find it easier to get into the rhythm of my body if I can shut off my mind.

T: After you got into the flow of the run by the river, then what happened?

P: I felt pretty good. When I came to the path by

the highway, all the cars were going bumper to bumper and I felt smug because I was moving faster than they were. And then some guy was sitting over by the side of the road with his Mercedes broken down and I really got a kick out of that. I was thinking: "Well, my body's better than your Mercedes. So there."

T: What else went through your head as you were going by, beside the fact that this big, twenty-thousand-dollar car . . .

P: That he was kind of cute and I wanted to offer him a lift. I was also thinking that jogging might not be so bad for my social life. That at least it would be an unpretentious way to meet somebody. I mean if someone said to you, "What do you do?" you wouldn't say, "Oh, my job is so and so." You'd say, "Well, you know! I'm *running*."

T: So you connect at a different level with someone.

P: Yes, and I like that. I went on ahead and passed a couple more men who were running very fast. One was really pumping and going along like a well-oiled machine. *Everything* on him was working, you could see that. What a great feeling that would be!

T: And you would like to have, but don't?

P: I get it in little bits when my stomach shuts up and my ankles stop hurting and I stop thinking of my muscles as those hateful things that are doing something underneath me. Then everything starts working together.

T: But you've been brainwashed to think that way. That none of that stuff is part of you . . .

P: I guess that was it. I was always called "the brain," which automatically implied that I didn't have a body . . .

T: By whom?

P: My family. My brother suffered from it as much as I did because he was "the jock" and I had "the brain." They sort of separated us like that.

T: How do you feel about the separation?

P: Really mad. I'm very bitter about that.

T: What do you recall about your body and the physical things you did as a child?

P: Up until I was about eight I felt very good about my body. And I loved being outdoors. My favorite part of the day was sunset. After racing and running around, I'd either climb a tree or lie down on the ground to watch the sun go down. And my mother would come out and yell, "What are you still outside for?" "Because it feels great. I love the ground. I love the earth. I love the sky. Leave me alone." . . . I just wanted to be by myself and run through the woods behind the house, down to the swamp and the school-house.

T: Did she bug you?

P: Mom wanted me to do other things. She tried to teach me to roller-skate. She was like everybody else who tried to teach me something. I was supposed to learn it her way instead of feeling what's in my body first and asking questions. That's what I like about running—there's no one telling me about "technique."

T: You've got a pretty free spirit. You don't want to be told what to do.

P: No—I rebel against that.

T: But you tell yourself an awful lot of things. There's one part of you that wants to be free, to run and jump and enjoy. And the other part of you is trying not to try . . .

P: Most of my life I've looked at it as a race. I've set goals and said to myself, "You're going to do it.

You're going to do it if it *kills* you." I make up for about a hundred other people telling me what to do. Then another part of me says, "I can't do this. Don't make me. I don't want to die." That's why I try not to push myself in my running. I'm trying to learn how to relate to myself, to my body. Instead of telling it what to do. I know what coming to grips with this can do for me, and I can't help thinking there are a lot of other people out there jogging, trying to do the same thing.

T: What do you mean—"coming to grips" with what?

P: With letting my body be taken away from me by social circumstances, social pressures. Then punishing my body in ways that I've punished it. Hating it the way I've hated it.

T: If I were to try and capture what you're after, it's somehow to reduce the separation you feel from your body and learn more about it? To be able to respect it fully and use it as an integral part of your living, rather than being dissociated from it.

P: Yes, and I want to get a lot of feelings back.

T: Then you have feelings that are "head" feelings and not "body" feelings?

P: I do—that's what I meant by trying not to try. In my running I lose that self-consciousness. I try with my body. I don't always want to live through *thought*—I want to begin to live through *experience*.

The resolution of any psychological problem is never purely intellectual—it is a physical and emotional event that demands the courage to take risks and an ego capable of enduring pain. Through running we learn to push past our preconceived limits, to endure stress, and to integrate the response of the body and the mind. If we overemphasize the power of the intellect, our growth takes place in fits and starts. The brain charges ahead, leaving a comet's tail of undigested feelings and emotions, and the body protests with aches and armorings in its effort to keep up.

If you are presently in therapy, you might try running to and from your weekly sessions—your body will bring your problems into focus and you won't end up sitting there with the usual blank expression, thinking, "Oh, God, so much has happened in the last week I don't know what to say." Running will lower your emotional resistances to the therapy and also provide you with a neat string of feelings and thoughts you're having here and *now*—you won't end up trying to describe how you think you *ought* to feel, but how you really do.

If you're not in therapy and want to explore the body-mind dialogue on your own, set aside some time for a therapeutic run. Try to be aware of every part of you as you jog, and when you come back, write down those areas you are more in touch with—where you have the aches or cramps—where you feel light and springy.

Then ask yourself these questions about your list:

1. How have I always felt about that part of my body?

2. What was happening when I began to notice it? What was I thinking, looking at?

3. What is the message from this part of the body? (i.e., Was I going too fast or trying to outrun myself? Was I feeling weak in the stomach because of something that happened this morning? Was there something someone said that made me feel powerless? Where did I go limp? Was I tense or angry as I ran? What happened to my body?)

4. What does it feel like in the body when you're happy as you run? What else gives you those sensations?

Start a jogger's journal and keep a record of these sensations—from aches and pains to pleasurable streamings and feelings of being perfectly centered within your own body. Take a few minutes after every workout to correlate these body sensations with your internal psychological state, noting what you were thinking and feeling before and during the run. (Later on you'll see how this journal can be expanded to include your dreams and the spontaneous images that pop into your mind as you run—and how this will enable you to delve deeper into your unconscious mind and explore your inner drives.)

You can take this particular exercise one step further, however, with the use of a large-format calendar. In one column note your physical activities during the day: sitting in front of your desk, traveling on the bus or train, jogging, eating, lying in bed with a book, etc. And in the next column write down those emotions and body feelings that characterize each segment of the day. You'll soon learn what your body is trying to tell you about each activity, and you'll shortly be aware of the nuances of body feelings and the meaning of body "cues"—knots of disgust lodged in the stomach, fear stuck in the throat, contentment evidenced by a suppleness and tingling in the limbs and deep, even breathing, tension deposited in the shoulders, any self-consciousness around the mouth or eyes. You'll notice that the more you move, the more you have pleasant body sensations, and the more sedentary you are, the more your body grumbles—and the greater the likelihood of your trying to pacify it with artificial stimulants, like cigarettes and caffeine, alcohol and food.

You'll also notice that you have more access to feelings and emotions when you run than at any other part of the day, and that you're beginning to expand your capacity for experience, your appetite for life.

How to Get Started: Some Practical Advice

It's extremely important to treat your body wisely and fairly when you first begin to run. If you haven't had a regular program of exercise, it's best to start gradually. If you're not sure how far you can safely push yourself, get a physical examination, preferably from a doctor who knows the benefits as well as the hazards of running stress.

Just a checkup is enough for most people under thirty-five. But if you're overweight and smoke a lot, your doctor will probably ask you to take an electrocardiogram. And he may put you on a low-cholesterol, low-fat diet for six weeks before you start to run.

How can you tell if you're overstressing yourself as you're jogging? First, you should be able to carry on a conversation with a companion (or with yourself!), even if your comments are reduced to static phrases. Next, you should know how hard your heart is pumping and be careful not to exceed 75 percent of your maximum cardiac output. You can determine this by taking your pulse before and after each workout and counting up the number of beats within ten seconds. Long, slow distance running should keep you within twenty to twenty-four beats per ten-second time frame. To determine your target rate according to your age and level of physical fitness, consult the tables below:

Physically Untrained Adults

Age	Ten-second target rate in beats
20	25
25	24
30	24
35	24

40	24
45	23
50	23
55	23
60	23
65	22
70	22
75	22
80	21
85	21

Physically Trained Adults

Age	*Ten-second target rate in beats*
20	24
25	24
30	23
35	23
40	23
45	23
50	22
55	22
60	22
65	21
70	21
75	21
80	21
85	20

Running Form: For a long slow distance running, your body should be as straight and upright as possible. Leaning forward is sprinter's form and should be reserved for short distances like the quarter mile or for special speed training.

Run with your arms loosely and comfortably at your sides, with your wrists at waist level. Relax your upper body, but don't slouch. You should feel your rib cage lifting up and away from your waist. And you may notice a bit of tension and pulling on the stomach muscles—that's where you get the extra support required to keep yourself from sinking into your girth the way you would into an easy chair. If your upper body tires quickly and you feel achy in the back and shoulders, add some extra sit-ups to your warm-up routine.

Watch how your foot strikes the ground. You should land gently on the heel and roll forward with a slight springing off the toes. Some people land clumsily with an audible "thud." Instead, take this opportunity to be aware of the contact of every part of your foot with the earth. There are more nerve endings in the foot than any other part of your body, so don't cheat yourself out of this subtle sensory experience.

You should also avoid superfluous movements: limp, flopping hands or arms interfere with the natural flow of the run and waste your valuable energy. In order to last over long distances of five to ten miles, you have to use your body as economically as you can. It helps to picture yourself gliding smoothly and evenly through space, and to imagine a cat-like inner tension that starts in your groin and lifts up through the top of your head, straightening the rest of your body into a graceful alignment.

Endurance Now, Speed Later: For maximum psychological benefits, you should walk, jog, and run to the best of your ability, for one hour three times a week. Doctors who prescribe running to alleviate depression and anxiety and therapists who use movement to explore body feelings all agree that something magical happens in the last half hour of the run that liberates positive emotions and leaves you with special insights regarding your self-image, your work, and personal relationships.

So, if you've got to stay moving for sixty minutes at a time, it's best to start out slowly. Most people push too hard at first, get winded, and then stop to catch their breath. But starting and stopping is harder on the body than keeping up a steady, even gait. If you set too fast a pace, sticking to a seven- or eight-minute mile for the first half of your workout and then come to a grinding halt, the body will protest. Lactic acid will build up in your muscles, causing an overall stiffness and making it difficult to get started up again. But novice joggers can easily avoid this problem. Just resist the temptation to rush through the first half of the workout, and ease into a slow, loping run, letting the body discover what rhythm is right for you.

If you feel yourself getting tired or fatigued, slow down *immediately*. You'll regain control of your breathing and your heartbeat will slow as you drop to a brisk walk or a bouncy jog. If you feel the urge to speed up, save it for the last few minutes of the run. When you have the energy to sprint the last lap or two, remember to bring the body back gradually to a resting state. Allow five minutes of slow jogging to cool down, and end with the same gentle pacing with which you began the run.

Warm-Ups and Cool-Downs: While the body has an internal gear system and needs at least ten minutes to warm up in the beginning of the run, you can smooth out the initial creaky stages by doing some warm-up exercises for about fifteen minutes before your workout. Do about fifteen sit-ups with your knees bent, in an unhurried fashion. Follow these with three minutes of toe-touching. Stretch long and slowly from the waist and never bounce. Move as gracefully as you can, breathing fully and deeply as you stretch.

To warm up your hamstrings and stretch out your tendons, try some "vertical push-ups" against the wall. Stand about three feet away from the wall. Hold your arms straight out and place your palms flat against the wall. Keep your heels firmly on the floor. Lean forward with your body straight and bend your elbows, as though you would do a series of "push-ups" against the wall. Do about thirty of these very slowly. And if you feel too much strain on your muscles, move closer to the wall *or* allow your heels to lift up slightly from the floor.

Next, sit on the floor with both legs straight out in front of you. Keep your legs together and bend your upper body forward over your legs. Grasp your ankles with your hands and pull yourself down until you've folded yourself neatly in half, your hands on your ankles, your elbows over your knees, your stomach tucked in, and your rib cage falling over your thighs. Hang like this for ten counts, then sit up straight for another ten. Repeat this five times. If you can't bend all the way forward and reach your ankles, don't worry. You're simply stiff and rusty and it will take you a few weeks to get limbered up. When you do this exercise, bend as far forward as you can, grasping your calves or holding onto your legs as far down as you can, and pulling your upper body as close to your legs as you can. Remember to breathe fully and relax, for relaxed muscles can stretch a lot farther than tense and tight ones.

Next loosen up your upper body with a few head rolls and shoulder shrugs. When you start to jog, be sure your jaw is loose. Don't run with clenched teeth, clenched fists, or clenched muscles of any kind, or you'll undo all the good relaxing stretching you've done. You should also repeat these exercises after you run to calm your body down.

Shoes and Running Surfaces: Running shoes must have enough support at the ball of the foot without crowding the toes—or you'll end up with "jogger's toe": a blister and a blackened nail from rubbing against the ceiling of your running shoes. When you buy shoes, you should keep in mind where you're going to run: for jogging over uneven surfaces you need a wide heel with traction that will protect against turned ankles and sprains. For a smooth, hard, even surface like cement, you'll want narrower, built-up heels with a cushion to protect against repeated impact.

Don't order shoes by mail unless you've tried on the brand and model first, or unless you can return them, and you have another pair of running shoes to use in the meantime if they're not a proper fit.

Clothes: If you don't have regulation gym shorts or a stylish warm-up suit and want to make do in the beginning, make sure your outfit is loose around the thighs and underarms; otherwise you'll suffer from fabric burns and painful chafing. Pure cotton is the best year-round material. It allows the skin to breathe in summer. If you put on two or three T-shirts for inclement winter weather, you'll trap your body heat in between the layers, keeping in the warmth.

Women: No matter what degree of liberation you profess, you'll befriend your bra again when running. Constant bouncing up and down is a strain on the breast muscles and can cause discomfort while you jog. Also, wear cotton underwear. You may incur a problematic yeast infection from working out in nylon briefs. And don't jump into high heels just after running. They stretch your hamstrings and tendons in the *opposite* direction and you increase the likelihood of leg cramps, especially if you stand for long periods of time.

Diet and Vitamin Supplements: Don't have a heavy meal less than two hours before your workout. Your body will protest with gas, cramps, and stomach pains, and you'll have that uncomfortable bloated feeling no matter what you've eaten. Try to consume less at one sitting and to nibble often instead—it's better for the digestive system, as well as for your jogging.

You'll also need to take one whole gram of vitamin C for every hour that you run, as added protection against muscle injuries. (Vitamin C is necessary for the health of our connective tissues and is needed to carry enough oxygen

THREE

Running Away from Depression

Like modern-day alchemists we are probing the metal of the body for the secrets of the soul. And as we decode the messages of the body we are scientifically proving what was common knowledge to the ancient Greeks: the muscle is the cradle of the recognizable mind. After twenty-five centuries, long-distance runners remain the classic representation of the Greek ideal—*mens sana in corpore sano;* they are now providing the first empirical link between the body and the mind as physicians view their biochemical makeup as the paradigm of health and the anchor for revolutionary studies of anxiety and depression.

The Biochemical Basis for Behavior

Dr. A. H. Ismail of Purdue University tested a group of middle-aged college professors and administrators after twenty weeks of moderate jogging and found that running changes the levels of glucose, testosterone, and catecholamines—substances in the blood that inhibit relaxation and have been identified with states of anxiety, aggression, and depression. After only ten weeks of running, these paunchy, sedentary academics evidenced the beginning of a subtle yet definite personality change. "They became more open and extroverted," Ismail reports. "And their whole demeanor seemed more stable and self-confident."

British researchers have found that fifteen minutes of jogging sends a shot of epinephrine into the bloodstream— instilling feelings of well-being and triggering a mild euphoria known as the "runner's high." Young adults are notoriously deficient in this hormone, which may prove to be the biochemical basis for happiness.

At Saint Luke's Hospital in New York, Dr. Edward Colt is comparing the body composition of distance runners with alcoholics and manic-depressives. This long-range project is designed to illuminate the physiological basis for psychosis and shed some light on jogging as a potential cure. Jogging seems to regulate intracellular-extracellular fluid exchange, which is probably mediated by hormones, and may offer a body-based cure for those disturbances thought to be purely psychological problems. Colt believes these hormonal changes may be responsible for the jogger's improved mood—for keeping on an even keel emotionally and maintaining a calm and easygoing frame of mind.

A further piece of evidence links the runner's adaptability to cold to his ability to handle psychological stress. Dr. Richard Dienstbier of the University of Nebraska notes that the runner's improved circulation gives him a warmer emotional disposition as well. "People with good cold tolerance see themselves as calmer and more easygoing and believe they are more in control emotionally," he explains. "They are even more likely to enjoy adventure and seek out suspenseful situations which may make others nervous and insecure."

While distance runners are the touchstones for radical research into the biochemical basis for behavior, they are prompting widespread changes in medical practice. Psychiatrists are now discovering that the body–mind equation works both ways: unresolved emotional problems can disrupt our physical topography, resulting in such psychosomatic disorders as "nervous stomach, muscle fatigue, and hypertension, yet a neglected body can also result in displaced feelings of anxiety and depression. The good news is that running provides a simple, effective, short-term and low-cost cure for the nerve-wracking side effects of modern life. A regular jogging program can combat feelings of powerlessness and instill faith in our ability to manage change as it counteracts the nagging physical symptoms of anxiety and depression.

Chasing Away the Sedentary Blues

We've long known about the psychological peaks reached by distance runners. "I have only to lace on my running shoes," says world class marathoner Ian Thompson, "and the kinesthetic pleasure of floating comes over me."

While E. M. Forster said these transcendental highs were the goal of every athlete, runners seem to achieve them more than others because they stress their heart and lungs at a constant rate, building the body's capacity for oxygen utilization. Running is guaranteed to bring on feelings of euphoria, and now doctors are prescribing jogging to their patients in the belief that these transcendental peaks will counteract depressive lows.

According to John Greist, a psychiatrist at the University of Wisconsin, running can chase away the blues and alleviate the symptoms of garden-variety depression in a shorter period of time than traditional psychotherapy, and many people with temporary symptoms might do better to jump off the analyst's couch and go out for a good cross-country run.

At least one in ten people suffer from mild but recurring bouts of depression, the kind that eventually goes away by itself. Greist was amazed when over one half of the outpatients at the university mental health clinic complained of irritating symptoms of depression—a rate five times the national average. Those involved in intense or unfamiliar intellectual activity need even more exercise than the average person in order to compensate for mental stress and strain—and, paradoxically, such people are the least likely to incorporate any physical activity in their busy schedules. Greist sent eight psychiatric patients out to run three times a week for a half hour to an hour at a time, and by the end of ten weeks, six had recovered fully from their depression. Though they never discussed their problems with a therapist and were asked to refrain from any talk of depression in the run, these joggers got better at least as fast as those who opted for traditional sedentary psychotherapy!

While the University of Wisconsin program suggests running may be an effective, low-cost mass treatment for our most common psychological complaint, the weekend jogging clinics popping up in major cities across the United States, from New York to San Diego, could well be the bases for the nation's first grass roots' movement in community mental health. Some of these informal running classes boast a circulating membership as high as 200,000—people who drop in and out not just according to their desire for physical coaching but according to their psychological needs.

Greist believes the self-imposed loneliness of the long-distance runner has beneficial healing effects: "Far from being an exclusively physical therapy," Greist explains, "running provides a solitude where emotional as well as physiological introspection and feedback can occur."

"Running gave me time away from my problems at school—from the difficulties I had with my friends and from the drudgery of pre-med," explains Fred, one of Greist's depressed students. "When I got into my body I felt like I was in a different world. And while running didn't solve my problems, it did give me a temporary feeling of relief—like an aspirin—and enabled me to solve my problems on my own.

Fred Hubbard was a twenty-year-old resident of Madison, Wisconsin, who didn't like the idea of going to college in the same town where he grew up and pursuing a major that his parents had preselected. After the ten-week running program, Fred made the decision to transfer to another school and change his major to biology. "When I first got to the university I thought I'd have nothing to look forward to but sleeping and studying. My brother had been pre-med and told me to expect a four-year grind. I forced myself to go to classes feeling that any moment I might burst into tears. But running taught me that no matter how much I have to do, I need to allow myself the time and opportunity to do something that makes me feel good."

Harriet Crane, a graduate student in psychology, came to the psychiatry clinic because, like Fred, she was disillusioned with the quality of academic life. While Fred worked himself up to the point of nervous exhaustion, Harriet's response was to withdraw, and most mornings she had difficulty getting out of bed. "The rest of the time I couldn't concentrate. I was so lethargic," she recalls, "that I didn't want to do a thing. When I went to the clinic and was offered a chance to try the running program, even then I had my doubts. I hated running in high school because there was always an unspoken competition and I'd expected more of the same. But I started out jogging slowly and the depression lifted dramatically in just a few weeks.

"When I went home over the spring break and felt a new bout of depression coming on, I ran around the block a few times. Just getting up to move was enough to make me see my problems were minimal and I was capable of working them out," Harriet explains. "Finally my parents and friends began to push me out to run if they saw me lying around too much."

What Harriet and Fred faced was the simple disillusionment of signing up for a long haul and finding out it wasn't going to be the exhilarating experience they had hoped it would be. How many of us come to the same realization with regard to our jobs or personal relationships and yet know we have to keep on going? What do we do when we feel there's no excitement any more, or that the texture of our lives will remain the same for weeks on end, and are plagued by feeling that "nothing will ever change"?

Jogging can help you through your cycles of depression and self-doubt, make you feel strong enough to reassess your situation, and enable you to think through the necessary change in the way you run your life. At first the physical sensations of running will quite simply distract you from your preoccupation with feeling sorry for yourself, from thinking too much and dwelling on your inability to solve the problem. Then, running combats the body feelings of sluggishness and fatigue, and releases the adrenaline component of anger—untended hostilities can build up to a paralyzing pitch and contribute to your overall depression. After a few weeks you'll also acquire a sense of accomplishment from your running which offsets the nagging feelings of "never being able to do anything right," and with your increasing competence you banish the secretly nurtured notion that life is at a standstill and things will never change.

Running also builds patience and the belief that you can change your condition with steady application and constant effort. Significantly, the people who don't stick with jogging therapy are the ones who push too hard and expect too much of themselves too soon. But those who stay with the regular running program are more self-accepting and soon develop a realistic time-frame for the solution of their dilemma. Finally, the overall improvement in your physical condition translates into a healthier self-image, and a positive outlook replaces the hollow ring of projected self-defeat.

While people who are severely depressed should not attempt to substitute jogging for the clinical wisdom of a trained psychiatrist, the average person whose flagging spirits need a temporary boost can benefit from psychiatrist John Greist's ten-week running program. The guidelines are simple, and once you find your body can be an ally and an antidote to depression and fatigue, you will never sit through another bout of the sedentary blahs again.

1. Set aside a minimum of thirty minutes and a maximum of sixty minutes, three days a week for ten weeks for your running therapy.

2. Walk-run-jog for thirty to sixty minutes in such a way that you are never gasping for breath. If you can sing to yourself or talk out loud while running, you are not going too fast.

3. Run in a way that feels natural to you. Most people land either on their heels or on their heels and toes at about the same time. (Running on the toes is fine for sprinting, but you can't sprint for thirty minutes. However, a few people are natural toe runners and should continue doing what comes naturally.)

4. If your legs become sore, increase the amount of walking you do, and decrease the running. Run for half the time you ran the previous day and continue decreasing your workout by one half until you are no longer sore.

5. Reasons to skip a scheduled "treatment day":

a. fever
b. broken bones
c. chest pain which increases with activity (consult your physician).
d. leg pain—when walking for thirty minutes makes it worse.

6. Once you've determined the amount of time that does not make you sore, and you've found a comfortable pace, begin to increase your time by 10 percent each week. Beware the temptation, however, to "run forever." Even in these early stages running causes euphoria, and exceeding your body's adaptive ability will surely lead to pain, fatigue, interruption of running, and a possible reinforcement of depression.

7. At any point after the third week, add a fourth day of running-walking to your prescription. If you are enjoying your jogs a great deal and missing them on the off-days, you may add another day a week, beginning with the sixth week. Do not add more than one day per week—and don't hesitate to drop back one or more days if you grow fatigued. Remember, though, that fatigue is a symptom of depression that can be relieved by running, so try very hard to run at least three times a week.

8. Keep track of the number of minutes you are jogging and record any special observations in your diary.

9. If you aren't feeling less depressed after ten weeks of running, consult your physician for alternative treatments for your depression.

It's also a good idea to make a definite appointment with an understanding friend and stick to the same regimen every day. Emma Parks, a thirty-five-year-old retailer with a business in her home, found she got so used to staying in that she couldn't force herself to get up and out of the house by herself. "My biggest problem was that I didn't want to move. So I made a pact with my neighbor, and once I'd been running for five minutes I knew I wouldn't quit."

When we are depressed, most of us have trouble getting out of bed in the morning. We simply need a reason to say to ourselves, "Come on, get up now!" So make a commitment to another person to run at the start of your day. Then, after the first six or eight weeks, you'll have built the cause-and-effect relationship into your body; you will retain a memory of the run that washes away your sadness and gets you going every day.

Anger and Hostility: Draining off Negative Emotions in the Run

Often we become depressed because we're taking our anger and hostility toward others and turning it against ourselves. Whenever Marge K. went through a dry social spell she soon began to berate herself for being unpopular and unattractive. The truth is, she was neither—she just had a way of shouldering the responsibility for all her past relationships. Finally she discovered a way to flush out her frustrations by holding imaginary dialogues with her ex-lovers as she ran. "If I went three weeks without a date, invariably I'd lose my perspective and think how terrific my old boyfriends were. Then I'd hate myself for having ruined those relationships—totally forgetting that there were special reasons that none of these affairs worked out." Like Marge, you might try turning your jogging into a rite of exorcism. Now when she feels these moods coming on, "I start running and go through every relationship in my head from the time I was twenty on, reminding myself of all the reasons that none of them worked out: Bill was too boring, Jim too selfish, John hated classical music, and Hal was going to spend the rest of his life traveling, while I liked to stay in one place. I'd go over our major disagreements and try to look at them objectively—and by the end of the run I'm *glad* I haven't compromised. I'm no longer feeling sorry for myself because I'm unattached. I've lost most of my hostility toward my past lovers—and gotten rid of negative emotions that kept me brooding by myself and that I might otherwise have unleashed on some unsuspecting date. Through running, I'm freeing myself from an old pattern. I don't feel powerless or think that nothing in my life has changed."

Jim T has always considered himself "high-strung"; he found that running could replace the large doses of tranquilizers he was taking to calm his monthly attacks of nerves. Jim recalls how he felt immobilized by anger when he was betrayed by a friend at a time when he felt particularly vulnerable. He explains how jogging enabled him to pull himself out of what could have been a major depression.

"I had introduced Bob to the vice-president of the advertising firm where I work and had given him a glowing recommendation," Jim recalls. "Both of us are well-known writers specializing in TV commercials—and I thought I was being magnanimous in opening the doorway for another hot-shot competitor. Later I found out that Bob negotiated a salary $5,000 more a year than I was making. And the way he'd gotten it was to tell the VP that he had more talent and experience than I! I felt like I'd been taken and couldn't get my mind off it.

"Two years ago I would have started popping tranquilizers in order to calm my nerves. I was so angry I couldn't concentrate on my work. I just couldn't stop thinking about it until I decided to go out and run. By the time I'd finished, I'd racked up ten miles—the longest run of my life—and I felt completely drained of all hostility.

If I hadn't gotten rid of all that pent-up anger, I would have stayed immobilized for the rest of the week and missed an important deadline—proving that Bob really *was* a more experienced writer than I!"

If we take tranquilizers to alleviate our pain, we may find ourselves falling deeper into a rut of unresolved emotions. As we allow the chemistry of drugs to act on us, without learning how to act ourselves, we increase our feelings of powerlessness. Many times the simple "garden-variety depression" tied to the inevitable ups and downs of circumstance is irritated by indiscriminate use of medication—or prolonged by inappropriate analysis of the problem. We can sit through a passive recounting of our woes and wait forever for some mobilizing insight to strike like a thunderbolt and hurl us back into the mainstream of our lives. Yet all we need may be the catalyst of movement to raise our energy level and enforce our feelings of self-mastery and physical control. Even the most active among us have times when neither work, nor love, nor money seems to flow to us at their accustomed rate. Running, quite simply, is a way of taking positive *action*—and of feeling that despite these lulls in our external affairs, we still remain the masters of our fate.

FOUR

Anxiety and Fear: Running to Control Your "Fight or Flight" Response

Primitive man had an immediate reaction to fear; he either attacked or ran away. And in running he was able to immediately discharge the physical swellings of his terror, the heavy heartbeat, the short and tensioned breath.

At the battle of Marathon in 490 B.C., the Greeks were outnumbered two to one by the infantry of Darius I. According to Herodotus, they adopted "a novel strategy." They *ran* at the Persians. But this was really a variation on an old familiar theme. The military reaction to anxiety is frequently an impetuous rush against the enemy—for the gasping, adrenaline-fueled attack diminishes the "charge" of an aroused nervous system.

Primitive religions also rely on running to lessen the anxiety of conversion. In Balinese rituals, for example, the excitement of the initiate is dispersed by exhaustive dancing —and the ceremony for rebirth consists of endless circle-running.

Today, whenever we feel threatened or experience a sudden shock, our genetically inherited "fight or flight" response is triggered. We receive a jolt of heart-thumping adrenaline which can be discharged through violent confrontation, or in the aggressive, pumping action of the run.

44

But we are no longer in the dry savannahs of our birth, and though we still retain our three-million-year-old instincts, it is socially unacceptable to react with florid rage —or to get up and sprint away. As we stand frozen in this netherworld of psychic immobility, unable to make a move toward emotional expression or physical release, what happens to the body's survival mechanism and our pent-up adrenaline charge? We suffer breathlessness and heart palpitations—the cardiovascular components of anxiety made from the physiological remnants of our running past. And the more sedentary we become, the more we fall prey to feelings of powerlessness and anxiety in stressful situations. Our anguish grows in direct proportion to our lack of physical control.

Anxiety and Breathlessness

People in poor physical condition are actually more afraid of not being able to breathe under stress than they are of the incident which triggers their anxiety. British psychiatrist Arnold Orwin has discovered that running can alleviate the distressing symptoms of anxiety and enable us to confront our fears rationally and control our physical response to danger.

According to Orwin there is a natural buildup of energy in the nervous system which manifests as anxiety unless discharged by strenuous cardiovascular activity. "Energetic activity is beneficial for releasing the tensions of everyday life," he writes. "Further, muscular action relieves anxiety by completing the fundamental biological pattern of arousal." This buildup of internal drive, then, must be released through regular activity such as running, or serious psychological disturbances will result.

Orwin first stumbled upon the running cure when he encountered a twenty-four-year-old patient with an unusual phobia about high-level lavatory tanks (the elevated basins are still common in British washrooms). At the age of two, Susan's mother led her into a dark public lavatory. The child was horrified by the sound of running water above her head. When she was nine, an aunt took her into another dank facility and forcibly placed her on the seat. Susan kicked and screamed until she was removed and thereafter refused to enter an unfamiliar lavatory with a high-level tank. The young woman now complained that her social life was considerably curtailed since she could only go out with friends who understood her terror of the basin dropping on her head!

During the initial therapeutic session, Orwin revealed to Susan that a tank had been placed on the ledge above her on the windowsill and concealed behind the draperies. At that point she ran from the room in a state of panic. "Then, as she recovered her breath," Orwin explains, "she discovered that the viewing of the cistern no longer produced anxiety, only a slight feeling of unease, which was quite endurable."

Orwin believes once the individual begins to run and feels he has the power to escape, his anxiety level lowers and his panic disappears. He has also used the running treatment with agoraphobics—people who fear walking through streets and open spaces. And his experiments have encouraged other therapists to apply the running cure to cases of claustrophobia and hypochondria. At the University of Washington, Drs. Bart Muller and Hubert Armstrong prescribed jogging for a Mrs. T, a forty-two-year-old woman who complained she was unable to accompany her husband on business or vacation trips due to her fear of riding in elevators. She reported shortness of breath, heart palpitations, and excessive perspiration, and added that she felt "weak around the knees at the prospect of entering the cramped and crowded space." Muller and Armstrong felt that jogging would enhance Mrs. T's feeling of physical control and give her a positive model for the management of cardiovascular stress. During the initial session, Mrs. T learned that she could control her breathing if she ran to and from her destination, and she immediately began to practice with a shopping spree in a nearby department store.

Learning to Trust Your Body

Psychiatrist John Greist used running therapy to cure a "cardiac neurotic," a forty-seven-year-old man with no history of heart trouble, who feared that at any moment he would die of coronary arrest. Jack L was considered a "low risk"—both his parents were in excellent health and over eighty years of age. Jack himself was never overweight, didn't smoke, and wasn't a particularly tense or nervous individual.

But when Jack's nine-year-old daughter came down with spinal meningitis, his fear of his own death increased to the point where he imagined himself clutching at his heart and being rushed to the hospital with a fatal attack. When a medical examination revealed nothing wrong with his heart, Jack went into running therapy and his fears abated as he learned to control his breathing and his heartbeat under stress. Greist had Jack continue jogging even though he complained of pains in his chest—and soon Jack found that these "symptoms" were the result of his irrational fears and were not biologically based.

The moral we can extract from these situations of exaggerated cardiovascular stress is this: if there is something you don't want to do, if you have a task that causes your heart to flutter and your lungs to contract at the mere thought of it, and you feel the usual clutching symptoms of anxiety, run before you have to do it. This can be anything from giving a speech to the board of directors of your company to going for a job interview.

Jane Levitt is a thirty-three-year-old English professor at Rutgers University, who arranged her teaching schedule so she had time to run before her first class every day. "Before I began running I was so terrified of teaching that some mornings I imagined my throat was closing up. I knew it was ridiculous. But it was the thought of being evaluated unexpectedly by the department head that made me a nervous wreck. I kept on thinking 'What if they drop in on me during an eight o'clock class when all the kids are half asleep even though I'm giving my most inspired talk on Shakespeare?' But, I always feel less self-conscious and more at ease after jogging," she explains.

Peter Crowe is a handsome, affable advertising director for a national news magazine, who confesses to a fear of being called on by the vice-president at monthly staff meetings. "Of course nobody knew how upsetting this was for me. I'd only had a few isolated occasions of this throughout my whole career—it's just a certain kind of ultra-authoritarian individual who brings out this fear in me. I'd start to breathe hard and perspire and imagine I was stuttering on every word. Fortunately the meetings are scheduled first thing in the morning or just after lunch. So I can run before I come to work or take my lunch hour at the track in the company gym. After having breathed all the fear and anxiety out of me, I feel 100 percent calmer during the meetings, and no matter how hard-nosed the VP gets, I can stay perfectly relaxed."

Our phobias often seem so embarrassingly ridiculous that we never admit them to our closest friends. Jason is a painter I've known for seven years, who only recently told me "fear" was the reason he started running. "In 1968 I went to Brittany to do a series of paintings and after a day of working at my easel in the bright summer sun, I came down with heatstroke at a café and fainted face down into a plate of snails at the hotel where I was staying. I've had such a distaste for the smell of garlic ever since that I have hurried past French restaurants and successfully avoided eating at any European café for years. But last year I was asked to design the wine list and the menus for New York's most fashionable lunch spot—of course, with French cuisine. I was so nervous I knew the only thing to do was to get to the initial meeting as fast as possible. So I put on a pair of loose wool pants and comfortable shoes and ran the fifteen blocks to the restaurant. For the first five minutes all I could think of was breathing deeply and evenly and making certain I was still presentable; I was completely unaffected by the plate of snails that passed in front of me. Now whenever I go there for dinner, I simply take a full-length jog first."

How to Use Running to Confront Your Irrational Fears

First, run as soon as possible after the initial fear impulse strikes. You want to establish a direct relationship between the fear and your ability to subdue your panic as you regain control of your heartbeat and your breath. Concentrate on your running—don't analyze your response. In this instance, insight will get you nowhere. What you need to do is develop a very real sense of self-mastery and physical control. Don't push beyond 75 percent of your maximum cardiac output (see the chart in Chapter 2) and try to keep a steady, even pace. Breathe deeply and concentrate on breathing *out,* not in. Most people stop breathing when they are afraid—they hold the air in their lungs, then struggle to let more air in. If you focus on the exhale, you will avoid this pitfall. Push the air out with an audible sound, "Ha!" You will automatically take in enough air to fill them up again.

Run for as long as it takes you to get your breath and heartbeat under control. Because this will probably take twenty minutes to half an hour, jog slowly and stay moving as long as possible. Run by yourself or with an understanding companion. If you take on a competitive running partner, you'll simply feel the added pressure to regulate your pacing and your breathing according to his demands. And in so doing, your physiological response will remain outside of your control.

Finally, if you run regularly—a minimum of three times a week—you will establish enough confidence in your ability to overrun the "fight or flight" response so that you will never experience an unnecessary and embarrassing urge to flee again.

FIVE

The Runner's High: Replacement for Negative Addictions

Running is our original biological means of draining off anxiety and tension. But what happens when we forget to use this built-in self-regulatory system for stress release? The body grows rigid in response to overwhelming internal pressure, and all our energies are directed toward keeping up a stoic pose. Our character and willpower weaken. We become overly self-critical and then begin to look for short-term solutions for our emotional pain. And this undis-charged anxiety and tension soon flow over into self-destructive behavior—such as the over-consumption of alcohol, drugs, cigarettes, and fattening foods.

According to psychiatrist William Glasser, people turn to such pastimes in order to elicit feelings of euphoria like those we experience naturally in the run. He calls these artificial highs "negative addictions" which bring momen-tary streamings of physical pleasure but ultimately dull and deaden us, for these pleasures are passively received. Ad-dicts have the right idea in trying to do something on a regular basis to make themselves feel good. It's just that they become dependent on artificial stimulants to do *for* them what the body should do naturally.

Running is man's biologically built-in means of self-gratification. It is a positive addiction which builds character, enhances individuality, reinforces long-term goals, and helps you kick whatever nasty habits you currently employ in order to feel good. "A good run activates our ancient neural program," Glasser explains, "and leads to a state of mental preparedness and brings on basic feelings of satisfaction." Then why do we turn to other methods of self-gratification when we can so easily trigger this pleasurable feeling as we run? By plying ourselves with alcohol, drugs, cigarettes, and fattening foods we can achieve a feeling of "fullness" and drown the ache and emptiness of our lives.

But the popular cures for all these negative addictions, which leave us feeling "hung-over," "groggy," "mealy-mouthed," or simply unattractive and overweight, all rely on what jogging provides naturally: improved circulation and respiration and a natural purification of the system through the flushing out of fluid wastes. Alcoholics may be fighting a basic fluid imbalance which running can correct. Smokers find the deep breathing of the run cancels the need for cigarettes. Moreover, overeating and taking drugs are simply shortcuts to achieving those oceanic body feelings that come naturally in the first half hour of the run. Then, too, jogging releases a morphine derivative in the brain, bringing us to a state of euphoria that far surpasses any artificial high—with no morning-after side effects.

Getting Strong:
Running Away from Self-Destructive Thoughts

Not only does running replace the physical pleasures we reap from our addictions, it also sets up the mind-set to kick these nasty habits and resist backsliding into destructive behavior. The addict is overly self-critical and invariably lacks faith in his ability to change. Yet jogging is less self-critical than any other activity we can do alone. As we run, we are distracted from the kind of unremitting self-analysis and dogged self-criticism which only serve to reinforce our negative addictions. Most of us—whether we be smokers, caffeine cravers, social drinkers, or icebox raiders —turn to these palliatives in order to quell some manic recounting of our own inadequacies. And we also don't believe we have the strength to stand up to our failings without a psychological crutch. But jogging can provide escape from this compulsive examination of our weaknesses. As we concentrate on the step-by-step of the run, we forget the litany of our flaws and allow the ego to repair. One woman confessed that each time she argued with her husband she ran to the refrigerator and consumed an entire loaf of bread, slice by slice. Now, instead of deepening her humiliation by a bout of overeating, she goes out for a three-mile jog. A former alcoholic reported that running quashed his desire to drink. He no longer needs a cocktail to drown the disappointments of his business day since he's discovered how to restore his sense of accomplishment through running.

While people with negative addictions generally don't have the faith in themselves to try and kick their habits, distance running quickly breeds unflagging belief in their ability to stick to long-term goals.

"The first choice of the weak is to give up," says Dr. Glasser. But runners never do. Marathoner Kathrine Switzer explains the leap of faith required to run the last leg of every race. "After twenty miles I make a bargain," she says. "God, if you lift the left foot, I'll take care of the right."

Through this self-confrontation you learn to laugh at your inventive excuses and become more accepting of your flaws while you develop the determination to push past them just the same.

"I decided it was time to stop drinking when I woke up

in my hotel room on a business trip and didn't know where I was," says John C whose running, in combination with AA, enabled him to kick a lifetime addiction to alcohol. "The first runs of my new life were very difficult. I had chest pains and stomach cramps, shortness of breath. I took the runs to be done with them. While I ran, I thought only about how good it would feel when I could stop. Then a little bit at a time, a moment here and there, I began applying parts of the AA program on running. I practiced living within the run, trying to accept where I was at that exact moment of my life. Gradually each run took on a separate life of its own. I felt better than I had in years. My body was getting stronger and the pain seemed less and life improved. Where I had been all alone in the hell of my addiction I now had new friends through running."

At the age of forty-two, John ran the Boston Marathon. "I knew this was the logical culmination of a daily program of *action*," he explains, "and through this program I was developing physical and emotional stamina, building my self-confidence and a whole new self-image. I learned about myself by confronting myself in every running workout. I looked at things I had been afraid to look at, things I had denied totally—and I wasn't disturbed by what I saw. At last I knew that the worst possible thing I could find out about myself was that I am a human being."

Negative addictions are not just limited to artificial stimulants, foods, and drugs that we ingest. Relationships which are self-destructive can be "negative addictions," too. Hal Kelly first used running to quell his desire for a drink ("If I don't run at five o'clock I still have difficulty resisting a martini"). But after he had pulled himself together, with the help of running and AA, he soon became entangled in a love affair that threatened his marital stability.

"Several months ago a young woman came into our

prayer group and slowly, almost imperceptibly, our relationship began to grow," Hal admits. "Finally, for the first
time during my marriage, I was unfaithful. The results
were terrible. I lost twenty pounds, my kids were shaken, I
had to leave the prayer group, and my wife, Alison, ended
up in the hospital with a nervous breakdown. Soon I
realized I wasn't happy with this woman, and I had to stay
away from her. It became apparent that more than anything it was a physical attachment. We didn't love each
other though the sexual pleasure I got from the relationship
was greater than anything I'd ever had before. Now I just
wanted it over, but I felt like a martyr—just like I had
when I was still carrying around this tremendous urge to
drink, and knowing that I had to give it up.

"When I had to resist going to her house, or calling her
up, it was just like driving past the gin mills. And I thought,
'My God, I'm going to go up the wall.' But every time I ran,
my compulsion drained out of me."

Running was a real leveler for Hal. It automatically took
away the obsession to phone his mistress, to fantasize about
getting a divorce, leaving his six children to pursue a woman
he knew he didn't really love. "It gave me a moment of
clarity," he sighs, "in what seemed to me an insane life."
Those long, quick runs allowed Hal to reassess his behavior, work through his physical hang-ups and needs for
sexual gratification, and brought him through the second
hardest battle he had ever had to get through in his life.

Learning to Give Yourself Pleasure

How often we stay in destructive relationships to provide
ourselves with physical pleasures, to give ourselves the illusion of being accepted and loved! What we seek with all
of these negative addictions is a feeling of transcendence,

an affirmation of the meaning of life, a momentary escape into an ether of security and well-being.

Until the recent interest in running and meditation as the paths to altered states of consciousness, the only culturally sanctioned ways to find the transcendental elements of life were through church or religious groups, through marriage or love relationships, or through total immersion in creative activity.

But, if you're not a member of a church or meditation group, if you're not having a love affair or getting positive feedback for your work, you no longer have to go without these feelings of self-affirmation and expansive ecstasy.

What must you do in order to establish this beneficial physical addiction?

1. First, run regularly—a minimum of one hour three times a week will establish you as an "addict" within six months. Running becomes habit-forming not only because it instills feelings of self-satisfaction and accomplishment, but because the body gets used to its natural high. "Hardcore" addicts need at least an hour of movement *every day*.

2. Next, jog or run in a noncompetitive manner and refrain from self-evaluation or self-criticism during the workout.

3. Run because you enjoy it and believe it's a valuable way to spend your time. Have faith that you will improve naturally, without strain or conscious effort.

When you reach the positive addiction, or PA state, all self-doubts and feelings of unworthiness disappear.

"It's a transcendental state you've earned," Glasser explains. Most of us feel guilty or suspicious when we suddenly feel good or happy—but we don't question the physical and psychological pleasure that we experience in the run simply because we've *worked* so hard to achieve it. And once you've been running regularly for six months you'll find you can't get along one day without it. This sensation of well-being is so intoxicating that we no longer need any other artificial stimulants to get there. If you miss a few weeks from your running, you'll even notice symptoms of withdrawal from your natural euphoric state.

Advice to the Injured Runner

What if you have to interrupt your running program because of illness or injury? Instead of returning to your old habits, you can substitute other forms of physical activity to satisfy your body cravings. If you're confined to the house with a cold, or if it's simply too late, too cold, or too hazardous to run, put on the wildest disco record you can find and dance for at least an hour straight. This is the closest thing to jogging that gets the breath and heart moving at an accelerated rate. If you've pulled a tendon or are recovering from a running-related injury, try swimming laps at the nearest Y. When you are just about ready to run again, switch to long-distance cycling to get your Achilles tendons back in shape. If you combine all of these exercises with five minutes of deep breathing in the morning, you can manage to avoid the worst pangs of withdrawal. But the simple fact of the matter is, there is nothing that works as efficiently as running to bring on the body's own organic high.

Dr. Glasser polled over 300 joggers to find out how they felt when they couldn't run. Complaints ranged from apathy, constipation, depression, guilt feelings, sluggishness, headaches, stomachaches, and fatigue. "There's nothing that will relieve that agony of not running," one serious runner explained. "Walking, biking, swimming, and sex are pleasant enough, and I speculated that one or two of them might be a substitute for a permanently ruptured tendon. But walking, biking, and swimming are to running what masturbation is to making love—only a bit better than abstinence."

"Sometimes I wonder—am I going to be doing this at ninety?" laughs Carol, a newspaper reporter assigned to investigate the nation's jogging craze, who caught the bug herself. After only eight months of running, Carol felt so good that she knew she'd never stop. In addition to that healthy glow, and the early stages of runner's euphoria, she experienced an overall elevation in mood. What Carol and others are feeling is simply the body doing everything right—flushing out the tension and anxiety of the day and establishing a biochemical balance and internal harmony. For marathoner Jim Fixx, this perpetual well-being has become a way of life. "The truth is, there is no runner's high," Jim explains. "It's just that everybody else is suffering from *non*-runner's low!"

SIX

Running Reborn: Jogging and Life-Style Change

Ever since we acquired the rotating femur—the architectural innovation that made man a natural distance runner, the biggest mistake we can make is to lapse into the viselike grip of a sedentary life-style. When we stop moving, we fall prey to all kinds of maladies, from hardening of the arteries and fatal heart disease to another form of lifelessness which anthropologist Ashley Montague calls "psychosclerosis"— a hardening of the mind and a form of premature aging which results from losing touch with the physical laws of change. Yet, if you jog regularly—as little as five or ten miles a week—you can soon regain those benefits which accrued to our mobile ancestors, and you'll find that almost unconsciously you've begun to radically alter your current way of life.

Rediscovering Your Biorhythmic Cycles

If you've been running for a while, you've doubtless experienced some of these physiological changes already, but if you're just starting out, here's an idea of what kind of transformations you can expect.

When we arouse the primal runner in each of us, the first thing we begin to notice is the reestablishment of our biorhythmic cycles. Primitive man was alternately vegetarian and carnivore, nocturnal and diurnal. He ate, slept, moved, and reproduced in different cycles, and a recent study of the patterns of animal and human behavior shows that a steady diet of anything is anathema to nature—and to man. The Kalahari bushman survives on herbs, fruits, and nuts until he successfully orchestrates a hunt—about once every thirty days. Then, as he feasts, his stomach bloats to four times the normal size, while his lean round rump fills out to astounding proportions. In the next thirty days he runs it off and again assumes his sleek lines, as well as his vegetarian habits. (The carbohydrate loading that many marathoners indulge in before a race is not so far from the Kalahari habit of feasting followed by the long run home.) Moreover, our bingeing, that inexplicable urge to overdo at the dinner table, may also be part of our ancestral eating pattern. What's so hazardous about our present diet is the tendency to eat too much *too often*. Anyone who's ever tried to run on a full stomach knows that he needs at least two or three hours of fasting first, and then the run seems to cancel the need for food and reduce one's appetite.

Napping in the afternoon is not uncommon for runners, nor was it, I suspect, for early man, particularly in the Pliocene, when it was to his advantage to stay out of the way of predatory beasts. The quality of sleep changes, too, and, as psychiatrist Kostrubala has noted, running seems to stimulate the unconscious and cause people to dream more vividly and more often. Runners also tend to take their sleep as they need it—in short naps—and to sleep more soundly at night for less time than they would require without the daily workout.

What essentially takes place as a result of running is a kind of inner attunement to the body's needs that replaces the arbitrary strictures of routine.

The reestablishment of cycles also extends to running, so seasoned racers frequently have less compunction about sticking to a daily schedule than rank beginners, simply because the more they run the more they need to recover. Tom Chandler, a forty-seven-year-old pathologist from southern California, runs five marathons every year in a nine-week period, from January to March. "I like to race this way because I experience more of a cycle," he explains. "I have a couple of weeks afterward where I can paint the house, tinker, and get other things done, before I have to start putting in the miles again." Running fast has the same effect. If you turn on the speed and exceed your usual pace, you'll cancel the need for another run until your body has rested.

Edward Dewey, president of the Foundation for the Study of Cycles, points out that there are thousands of rhythmic cycles about which we know almost nothing. "These forces bind us like marionettes on a string," he writes. "They make us fight. They make us love. And all the while we think we are doing these things for solely rational reasons."

One of the lessons of the body is that we were not meant to function like statistical charts, consuming so many calories per day, making love so many times per week, or running so many miles in fourteen minutes every single day. When we attune ourselves to the rhythms of the daily run, we begin to be aware of the larger biorhythmic shifts in other aspects of our lives.

Running Away from Heart Disease: The Number One Killer Is Your Sedentary Life-Style

While we can improve the quality of our lives by tuning in to the seasons of the body and to our own natural cycles, with a regular running program we can increase the likelihood of living a longer life as well. Since running is the prime genetic characteristic that made man more durable to begin with, it's only logical that a runner's life-style would contribute years to our life expectancy and protect us from the number one killer in a sedentary civilization: coronary heart disease.

The first documented case of heart failure occurred 1,600 years ago in a province of northern China. Doctors recently X-rayed and performed an autopsy on the remains of a Chinese woman, approximately fifty years of age, whose body was preserved in an herbal shroud. They were able to determine that she died from heart failure shortly after eating. She was also considerably overweight, and from the elaborate way that she was buried, there is every indication that she lived the typically affluent, sedentary life-style that today makes one out of two Americans a prime target for cardiovascular disease.

The good news is that runners make those changes in diet and in life-style which protect them from this cultural phenomenon.

The life-style factors that lead to coronary heart disease are a diet high in fats and high in cholesterol, obesity, over-consumption of alcohol and cigarettes, and lack of exercise. People who have no outlet for their aggressions and who haven't learned to handle stress have typically "Type A" personalities and are also more likely to be the targets of cardiac arrest.

Dr. Thomas Bassler of the American Medical Jogging Association makes the medical claim that marathon running can make us "heart-attack proof" for at least seven years. For once we start to run in earnest, we automatically lose weight, change our diet and smoking habits, drain off tensions, and instinctively begin to do everything right.

People over thirty-five who haven't had a regular program of exercise should first have a treadmill and electrocardiogram done to determine the amount of jogging their hearts can accommodate. And remember, running *alone* is not enough to make you heart-attack proof. Herman Hellerstein, a cardiologist at Case Western Reserve, himself a recent convert to jogging, cautions, "There's no data worth a damn to show that exercising sloppy, overweight, cigarette-smoking, paunchy men will make a bit of difference in their immunity to coronary heart disease."

However, Bassler's statement that running protects you against heart disease is limited to immunity from arteriosclerosis—the type of coronary heart disease caused by fat deposits—not by sudden shocks to the heart.

And he also makes the following qualifications: Jogging combats heart disease (1) if you do not train competitively. Running and racing to win breeds a Type A personality—aggressive, tense, and self-conscious, with an overriding concern to come in first and be in absolute control, and that works against the mellowing effects of a long, leisurely run; (2) if you have taken one year to train and have worked up slowly and gradually to your first ten-mile race; (3) if you're one whose running is a "positive addiction" and you work out nearly every day; (4) if you have given up smoking, hard liquor, and overeating because these habits interfere with your training program; and (5) if you're stalwart enough to have successfully completed the full marathon distance of 26 miles, 385 yards, with the intent to finish, not with the competitive urge to "win." Bassler himself runs marathons just for fun, stopping for a cold beer every couple miles. Once he checked his watch at the eighteen-mile mark and saw he was about to finish in less than three hours. Bassler groaned, "What the hell am I doing this for?", slowed his pace, and came in with a time of 3:11, a "personal best" he refers to as an accident.

Of course, the more you run, the more you'll be moved to change your diet and give up smoking and alcohol. Yet there is a point past which the body begins to break down and you begin applying unnatural stress. The first running-related injuries, such as sprains, strains, and pulled tendons, occur when you go over thirty miles per week. Generally those who do not spend at least twenty minutes before each workout doing simple stretching exercises for their Achilles tendons are most prone to these afflictions.

After the forty-mile mark per week you move into the competitive marathoner's league. While many of these super-distance runners tend to overtrain, racking up seventy-five to a hundred and twenty-five miles a week, such compulsive training won't make you immune to Type A tensions. Nor will it necessarily improve your performance. The way to get maximum psychological benefit from running is to enjoy every workout without becoming fanatic about your mileage.

If you're currently doing marathons, Bassler suggests you take this periodic test: "If you can jog ten miles, get along on 500 calories a day, and keep your sense of humor, you're in good working order. If you fall apart and get irritable under the strain, you should take a good hard look at the rest of your life."

Those who aren't "purists" and who haven't completely kicked their more decadent habits can at least soften their nefarious effects. If you still persist in smoking, you'll at least flush the toxins through your system faster by running. If you succumb every once in a while to one too many, there's nothing like a morning jog to get rid of that nagging hangover and clear the head. And if you tend to overeat, you can always step up your mileage to burn those pounds off to the tune of 100 calories per mile.

The Prevention Diet:
Bringing the Body Back to Normal

If you've already got heart problems, it's wise to listen to Nathan Pritikin of the Longevity Institute in Santa Barbara, and start reducing your fat and cholesterol intake *before* you begin a regular jogging program.

Pritikin studied the diets of the Bantu African tribes who show a low incidence of coronary heart disease, eat less than 10 percent of their calories in fats, and cover over 10 to 25 kilometers per day on foot. According to Pritikin, running and a low-fat/high carbohydrate diet are precautions that will (1) decrease your chances of clogged arteries; (2) increase collateral circulation—the functioning of small blood vessels near the heart; and (3) help speed oxygen through the body to feed the muscle tissues. Pritikin calls running "the ultimate exercise and man's healthiest activity," yet he points out that if you've been eating the equivalent of a cube of butter every other day and are billowing around the beltline, you should change your diet beforehand to avoid breaking off a "plaque"—a fatty deposit in the arteries—that could wend its way toward the heart.

The prevention diet recommended by the Longevity Institute consists of 10 percent total calories in protein, 10 percent in natural fats, and 80 percent in complex carbohydrates—food as it is grown and not refined. The prevention diet lowers your profile of cholesterol and triglycerides. Moreover, carbohydrates are the best fuel for running because they burn "clean"—producing carbon dioxide, water, and glucose. Fats burn only 85 to 90 percent and the rest is left in *ketones,* which can pile up in the blood causing fatigue and lethargy.

If you need to lose weight before you start jogging, try

restricting yourself to 600 calories in carbohydrates per day. According to Pritikin, you can lose up to twenty pounds in thirty days without artery damage on this diet. Though you'll instinctively start eating foods that will make you run better after the first six months of your training, you can get a jump on better running right away by cutting out the junk food and relying on high-energy snacks and a mainstay of lean meats, eggs and fish, fresh vegetables, and salads.

Run Longer—Live Longer

As we begin to use our bodies more efficiently, we may even be able to jog our way to a longer life. The American Medical Jogging Association has even found evidence that there is a parallel aging of the Achilles tendon and the coronary arteries, which means that all the connective tissues in your body are about as young as the muscles in your legs. But in addition to securing a strong heart and firmer muscle fiber by running, we find we also have something more to look forward to: increasing physical proficiency!

Running is the one activity that we get better at with age. Twenty-four-year-old Frank Shorter won the marathon gold medal in the 1972 Olympics in two hours, twelve minutes and nineteen seconds—only to be bested two years later by a forty-one-year-old New Zealander who turned in a time that was faster by a minute and two seconds. Eighty-eight-year-old Eula Weaver, who suffered a near paralyzing stroke ten years ago, recovered by jogging three miles every day and recently took a gold medal at the Senior Olympics track meet. Larry Lewis worked as a waiter at San Francisco's St. Francis Hotel and ran eight miles to work every day until he died at the age of 105 of an undetected infection of the gallbladder.

The darling of the Dolphin South End Runners Club in

San Francisco is a seventy-year-old construction worker named Walter Stack, whose body is as hard as an andiron and whose lean, tanned musculature sparks with nonstop activity. Stack swims for thirty minutes in San Francisco Bay, then jogs seventeen miles before he bicycles to work as a hod carrier, and he claims he's running better every year.

What is age but a bracing against change and a closing off of the innermost self to the vital forces of life? As we run we combat crankiness and senility and "a hardening of the mind, by sending extra blood and oxygen to the brain. By keeping up the prime occupation of our early childhood, we are doing what anthropologist Ashley Montague says is essential to staying young: we are retaining our capacity for new experience and prolonging our ability to absorb new information, physiologically, biologically, and psychologically in the time capsule of the run.

"People age prematurely," according to Montague, "because they are unable to embrace new ideas and because they continue to mistake their own prejudices for the laws of nature."

Through running we stay in touch with our own biorhythmic changes and establish a system of physical feedback that tells us when we're getting stronger and alerts us when there's something wrong. We learn that we don't have to give in to an "early retirement" of the body and that activity is the key to halting and reversing what we have commonly regarded as the necessary impediment of age.

By some ironic twist of fate, I happened to be running with George Leonard, a fifty-three-year-old author of *The Ultimate Athlete,* and black belt master of aikido, on the day that Robert Maynard Hutchins died. Hutchins was the one who said, "Whenever the urge to exercise comes over me I just lie down until it goes away"—and a man whose final supine gesture coincided with the running revolution and a cultural reawakening to the psychologically restorative values of sport. As we ran through the mountain trails near Leonard's California home, he told me with an air of dignified amazement, "I can do things now physically that I couldn't do at twenty-three"—expressing not only one man's liberation, but a whole generation's rediscovery of regular endurance training as an antidote to Hutchins's Victorian notion of the proprieties of age.

Jogging and Personality Change

California has long been thought of as the social laboratory of the nation, the place where *change* is not the exception but the rule. There most people have had their best job, marriage, or affairs by the time they're thirty-five or forty, and when the aura of their early success starts to wane, they begin "to die." It's not surprising, then, that California has spawned "running therapy"—actually a form of adult play which teaches people how to *recapture life*.

When San Diego psychiatrist Thaddeus Kostrubala started a group of patients jogging in 1973, he found that running is a natural cleansing experience that eases the anxiety and tensions which accompany major life transitions. At the same time, running activates the deepest drives of the unconscious, promoting psychological rebirth and acting as a catalyst for full-scale personality change.

"Most people who come into therapy want to make big changes in their lives," says San Diego psychiatrist Kostrubala. "Then they sit around and talk for months on end and nothing happens. You have to give people a prescription for change: run for a minimum of one hour, three times a week."

But that's not all that Kostrubala does. He actually goes out and runs *with* them!

Kostrubala has revolutionized the role of the sedentary psychiatrist offering analytic interpretations at a safe distance from the turmoil and conflict of his patients. Instead he leads his charges into the psychic area, enduring the heat and sweat of the roads and hills, and indicating to reticent believers that the modern physician must still be willing to apply the principles of transformation to himself. He believes this sharing of the run builds a basic trust and expedites the formation of a therapeutic alliance and subsequent cure.

"At the age of forty-two I found myself a member of that cult which attempted to fill the shoes of shaman, priest, and physician," Kostrubala explains, "but in the operating theater of the therapist's office the emotional voltage was in the kilowatt range, while the physical outlet of energy was in the microerg category. At least the shamans danced, priests moved about at their ceremonies. But the psychotherapist was sedentary."

Just as the body and the mind are engaged in the process of the run, the psychic responses of the patient and the therapist are also intertwined. Understanding is visceral, nonverbal, and immediate, and far different from the kind of communication we experience in the rest of our lives on the purely conscious level.

You don't have to be in therapy, however, to experience psychological rebirth in the run. Most joggers find that after several weeks of training they've already begun to undergo a subtle yet definite personality change.

If you're just starting out, what kind of changes should you expect?

1. First, an almost immediate boost in self-confidence related to your improving physical condition.

2. Next, more energy to invest in work and new creative projects. As a result of this new vitality you may even make

long-wished-for career changes. Increased imaginative abilities and self-motivation also come with a regular jogging program, and many people switch to jobs that will allow them more independence and greater control of their time.

3. You'll find you're most happy when you're active and will take up other sports, such as distance cycling, hiking, and mountain climbing that will draw on your added physical endurance, satisfy your craving for adventure, and enable you to spend more time out of doors.

4. As you reevaluate your personal relationships in the light of your newfound body-wisdom, you'll find you're no longer fascinated by people whose idea of a good time is staying out late and closing the local bars, and you'll slowly begin to change your circle of friends. A feeling of stronger bonds and a special kind of intimacy develops among runners by virtue of their shared commitment to a new way of life—one that includes eating health foods, sleeping well, spending more time out of doors, and building a physical base of creative and emotional expansion. Kathy Moore, an athletic divorcée in her thirties found in just the first eight months, "My life became centered around the physical and social joys of running and I found deeper friendships than I ever had before."

5. Because they're running closer to self-fulfillment, joggers also sense a guiding purpose in their lives and you may ultimately develop a renewed interest in religion. "Running's made me more of a Jew," says Steve Schwartz, a San Diego runner who's preparing for his bar mitzvah now, at age forty-eight. A jogging nun uses her morning workouts as prayer time; an essentially earth-worshipping cult has formed around the San Diego Marathon Clinic, based upon the Sunday morning ritual of the run.

Running therapy is filled with evangelistic stories, and Kostrubala's own transformation at age forty-two was brought about by running. Kostrubala, who weighed 230 pounds and was diagnosed as a "high-risk" coronary candidate, joined a jogging program designed to rehabilitate those in his condition. Now sixty pounds slimmer and a veteran of seventeen marathons, his inspirational model ("Physician, heal thyself") attracts more than 500 suburbanites every week to his *Sunday morning jogging clinic.*

As he jogs over the San Diego mudflats with his bamboo running stick, Kostrubala seems to have sprung from some ancient, animistic landscape of tree spirits and wood nymphs, a world still inhabited by Pan. With a shaved head and searching eyes that devour his surroundings with the deftness of a lizard swallowing a fly, he appears a strange combination of evolving cerebral consciousness and the archetype of primal cunning. The Jungian psychiatrist is a compendium of mythological heroes. *Holiday* magazine selected him "Youth of the World" as he was being routed into the heaviest combat zone of the Korean War. He reappeared as "Blackbeard"—a sailing aficionado with an oddly rural psychiatric practice on the Maine seacoast. Later he became one of Chicago's most brilliant analysts, an impressive figure in long white "Freud" suits. And after successfully treating schizophrenics, alcoholics, and manic-depressives with running therapy, Kostrubala has been hailed "the Moses who will lead people out of the mental hospitals and into the fields." His experimental unit at San Diego's Mercy Hospital is the only clinic in the country where you can't tell the doctors from the patients—everyone's wearing jogging shorts and running shoes.

Perhaps as a result of his own epic incarnations Kostrubala finds it easy to inspire far-reaching personality and life-style changes in his runners. A grocery clerk recently walked twenty miles from his home to Billings, Montana, to purchase Kostrubala's book, *The Joy of Running,* hiked to Utah, boarded a plane, and deposited himself at the doctor's door. The mother of a sixteen-year-old schizophrenic called to say that two years ago her son had started running spontaneously—she'd heard about the "running cure" and wished to bring him in. At the same time a couple left Anchorage, Alaska, to camp out in San Diego until Kostrubala agreed to run with them. Running therapy seems to have the appeal of a panacea, offering the hope of rebirth to people from all walks of life—from businessmen, housewives, divorcées, and teen-agers, to retirees and members of the clergy. There is an evangelistic fervor at these Sunday morning jogging clinics. And people place a fundamentalist faith in the power of the run to ease away their troubles and bring about a physical rebirth that spills over into the rest of their lives.

Now entire families assemble at 10:00 a.m. for the weekend marathon clinic at Mission Bay to jog two, five, eight, ten, and even twenty miles. The atmosphere is quiet and conversation hushed. And in the first few minutes of running, people concentrate on the sound of the footsteps, or count their breaths, in Zen fashion, focusing on the inner spaces of the run.

While in San Diego I ran with several of Kostrubala's patients, who were "regulars" at these Sunday runs. Each workout lasts approximately six miles, roughly the equivalent of the therapeutic hour, while the rhythmic footfalls on the pavement seemed to trigger a burst of enthusiastic self-analysis with the regularity of Pavlov's bells.

When I met Jim K, an engineer and inventor in his early forties, on an overcast morning at the surfers' beach in La Jolla, the sky was a dull, pearlized gray, the air crisp and chilly on our skin. As soon as we hit the beach, his life story poured from him like sand seeping through an hourglass.

"I was raised in an orphanage and spent my life becoming successful," he told me, "so I could insulate myself from the problems of life. I was president of my high school class, the star basketball player, and went to Harvard on a scholarship. By the age of twenty-six, I had my own business with forty-five people working under me. By thirty, I'd made a million. I'd married early and had four kids, and things were fine at home—but *I* was never there."

"Is this too fast for you?" he asked considerately. At five feet seven, Jim was a jaunty runner. He had just finished his second marathon. I was so fascinated by the candid confession from a stranger that I hadn't noticed the somewhat brisker pace.

"By age forty I started to look at myself. My work no longer was enjoyable. I kept redesigning the same piece of machinery over and over again. The project should have been a snap. But I couldn't seem to find the energy to invest. Then depression hit me like a wave. I sold my business, and two weeks later on vacation cracked up in a hotel in Santa Barbara. I realized I had never spent any 'quality' time with my kids, that I'd virtually ignored my family.

"Then I started running. At first my wife was suspicious. She thought the idea was crazy and that Kostrubala was a real home-breaker. But my creativity went up—running is terrific for problem-solving because it pares you down to the essentials. And soon I had more energy. I went back into business again, but this time I thought more about my family and less about buying things. Running also made me less of a materialist—I don't cart along anything that I can't put on my back when I leave the house to run, and instead of getting another family car, we've started jogging the five miles from the apartment to our beach house.

"Finally my wife started running when she was going through her own mid-life changes. She gave German and piano lessons from the house but she needed to get out and away from the home. Last week she did her first marathon at Palos Verdes, and finished—even though she had to walk the last eight miles."

Running gave Jim the self-confidence and stamina needed to get through one of the toughest transitions of his life, to renew his relationship with his family and his creative drive. As he became sensitive to his emotional needs based on the body feelings of the run, his obsession with material security decreased. He began to share his time with his family instead of "insulating" them with his money and depriving them of himself. His marriage improved, and as his wife noticed the beneficial influence of Jim's jogging, and his new expansiveness, she took it up herself.

Carol had only been running six months when I met her at Kostrubala's Sunday morning jogging clinic. We took the eight-mile loop around the island and she explained how just eight months ago she'd been depressed and confined to the house with the responsibilities of managing a corporate move. "When my husband was transferred to San Diego from Chicago, I gave up my job, my family, my season tickets to the opera and the theater. I had a hard time adjusting to suburban life and spent most of my time at home alone unpacking crates and feeling sorry for myself because I had no interests and no friends. Finally I decided to do something that was good for me so I began running on the beach two miles a day, and then found out about a jogging group at the Y. Now I run ten miles with two new friends on Tuesday afternoons through the Torrey Pines. I even get up at 6:00 a.m. for a jog around the block and it gives me more energy to cope with the house and the kids.

"As a result of the move, my husband and I started arguing, and I felt all bottled up. Finally, I went to Kostrubala and began to talk about my marriage in running therapy, and as we jogged and I talked, it became apparent that this was a destructive relationship for me. I wouldn't be able to express some of the feelings I've kept tucked away for so long without my running. I've only been in therapy for two months and already I've separated from my husband, gotten a new job, a new boyfriend, and started feeling more secure—big things for me."

Running lowers psychological inhibitions, and as Carol jogged she became more outspoken and assertive, and found her running had a consciousness-raising effect. She was able to define her needs to her husband, and when he refused to compromise, she asked him for a legal separation. And while Carol had formerly depended on her parents to get her through financial and emotional transitions, she was also determined to orchestrate the separation on her own. "I know I'll keep on jogging for the rest of my life," she explains. "It's my way of taking care of myself."

Running is guaranteed to cause such a difference in behavior that some people have even decided to drop out of Kostrubala's therapy because they couldn't tolerate the side effects of personality change. Unlike Carol, many do not want to risk altering their marriages, relationships, and jobs to suit their developing persona. When an accountant in his fifties, who had appeared rather taciturn at home, terminated his jogging therapy, he explained, "It's breaking up my marriage. My wife doesn't like the *new* me." She had married a shy, conservative type and didn't know how to handle the outspoken and gregarious runner she had suddenly acquired. Feeling forced to choose between disrupting his homelife or maintaining the veneer of stability in his relationship with his wife, he balked at the opportunity to change and literally refused to take another step in that direction.

While inner-directed running inevitably causes hidden

emotions to surface, how can we tell whether these forces reinforce our present life-style or begin to drastically shake us up? What determines whether running has an organizing or *dis*organizing effect on your present situation? First you must remember that running brings the deepest desires of your unconscious up to the conscious level. Hence any relationship that is based on instability or "lies" mutually agreed upon will begin to break apart. Those which are based on *real* needs and mutual understanding will begin to grow and flourish. If you use your running to open this trapdoor to the unconscious, you will automatically begin to rearrange your outer life according to the dictates of the inner drives. This can be both an exhilarating and painful process, depending on how well matched your life-style is to these inner needs and how much flexibility and psychic space you allowed yourself for change.

No one was more surprised than Kostrubala when, after his wife started running, his own marriage broke up. "We had the major emotional settling of our relationship during the Culver City Marathon in 1976," he admits. "Ann and I cried and argued and fought and wept for the full twenty-six miles and from then on we knew what was going to happen and so proceeded to work toward an amicable divorce."

While some people may experience a temporary disruption in their lives after they start to run as a result of acting from a deeper level of the psyche, others find that running has an immediate stabilizing and calming effect. People who are unstable to begin with report that running makes them psychologically stronger—and it's even brought about a positive reorganization of the personality, proving effective in such dramatic disorders as schizophrenia.

When Mary S came to Kostrubala six years ago, she had dropped out of graduate school, had been hospitalized as a schizophrenic, and spent a year on Thorazine. "I was always mentally hyped up and unable to concentrate," she explains, "until I started running. Then somehow I relaxed." At that point, Kostrubala, who was just beginning to experiment with jogging on his most difficult cases, "eureka-ed," "That's it! Cut back on your medication and run more." After six months of running for an hour every day, Mary's manic flights into fantasy had ceased, her hostility had been drained off in the run, she no longer needed drugs and was well on the road to recovery.

SEVEN

How Running Unravels
the Mysteries
of the Unconscious

While you may think that nothing's happening to you as you run, your internal structures are being subtly rearranged. You obtain a power charge that runs from the psychic core up to the conscious level and evokes childhood memories, uncovers secret goals and unarticulated wishes, inspires vivid fantasies and dreams, and illuminates the interior framework of the soul, laying the foundation for far-reaching psychological change. This process is so powerful and unique that we need an entirely new set of suppositions about the origins of man in order to explain it.

A New Model of the Psyche

Dr. Thaddeus Kostrubala has thrown some light on the way jogging reaches into the cauldron of the unconscious and activates our deepest drives with his theory of Paleoanalytic Psychology. Paleoanalytic refers to the biological evolution of man as a distance runner and the parallel development of certain psychological structures and states of mind. According to Kostrubala, what happens to the psyche during the run is analogous to our physiological develop-

78

ment in the womb. While the human embryo goes through stages of genetic evolution where it appears to have gill slits and then a tail, as we run we also recapitulate 3.5 million years of psychic development. It's as though we begin to peel away different layers of consciousness, reaching from the present back through our childhood (the personal unconscious), to our inherited genetic characteristics (the beginning of the collective unconscious), and finally back to our running ancestors and primal man.

Just as the body adapted to specific conditions of the environment during the long span of our evolution, so the psyche, too, has added certain functions which correspond to physical events. Kostrubala believes that man evolved psychically as he began to run longer distances, and that there is a direct correlation between developmental layers of consciousness and the amount of time we spend running. The first or most recent layer, "self-consciousness," is penetrated within the first twenty minutes of the run, and thoughts related to the self-image and body image are triggered. The second layer, ordinary consciousness of day-to-day events, is stimulated after thirty minutes. Tension and aggression are poured out in this phase of the run. Next to be activated is the personal unconscious, the main terminal for all events that have occurred within our life-style, including past associations with parents, lovers, and friends. Finally what Jung referred to as the collective unconscious, all inherited familial, ethnic, and genetic traits, is unearthed, in the forty to sixty range. This is where archetypal experiences, hallucinations, and waking dreams are released. According to Jung, the collective unconscious contains the whole spiritual heritage of mankind, born anew in the brain structure of every individual. Kostrubala extends this to include a basic resonance with the first runners, and back through to our animal and prehuman ancestors, and even

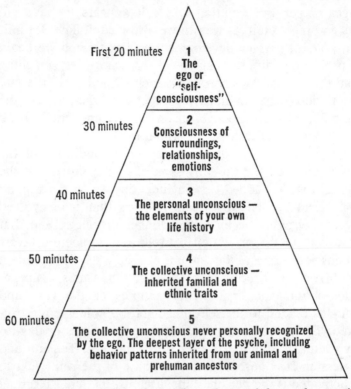

First 20 minutes / **1
The
ego or
"self-
consciousness"**

30 minutes / **2
Consciousness of
surroundings,
relationships,
emotions**

40 minutes / **3
The personal unconscious —
the elements of your own
life history**

50 minutes / **4
The collective unconscious —
inherited familial and
ethnic traits**

60 minutes / **5
The collective unconscious never personally recognized
by the ego. The deepest layer of the psyche, including
behavior patterns inherited from our animal and
prehuman ancestors**

According to Kostrubala, these different layers of the psyche are stimulated during the run in a strict time sequence. In the first twenty minutes of the run, we're focused on our self-conscious aches and pains and those ego-centered concerns for wanting to improve our bodies to begin with. After thirty minutes, we begin to muse over events in our work or personal relationships and to go over those life problems we already have consciously defined. After forty minutes, we begin to tap into the unconscious and resurrect memories and related emotions from the past. After fifty minutes, we draw on the collective unconscious, and on those psychological characteristics we've genetically inherited, related to our familial and ethnic background. Finally, after an hour, we evoke those elements of the psyche of which we are consciously unaware. Unbeknownst to us, we begin to activate those evolutionary psychic structures which made man different from his prehuman ancestors and to resonate with the deepest layers of the unconscious mind.

feels that there is another layer that goes back to the genesis of the earth and all forms of living consciousness.

Resonating with Your Unconscious in the Run

There are certain optimum conditions for resonating with the deeper layers of your unconscious as you run. First, you must begin your workout with an "inner-directed" activity that will take your mind off "sightseeing," other joggers, and mundane thoughts about your surroundings. You can count your footsteps or concentrate on the rhythm of your breathing. You can chant a mantra or the words to a favorite song, or even compose an inner prayer regarding your present situation. It is best to run alone and along a familiar path, so you won't be drawn into conversation or surveying an unknown landscape, and away from the meditative aspects of the run.

Competitive considerations (comparing yourself with others, or trying to best your own best time) will definitely distract you from the internal process of the run.

What is *key* is the amount of time you spend in motion, not the distance or the speeds of the workout: keep going at your best pace for about an hour. Stop and walk if you have to, but as soon as you're able, pick up to a jaunty jog. Kostrubala advises his runners to work at 75 percent of their maximum cardiac output, or 25 percent less than the heart is actually capable of pumping without strain. This puts you in a relatively slow, relaxed lope with your heartbeat ranging from twenty-three to twenty-five pulses every ten seconds. (See Chapter 2 to figure out your target rate.)

Next, remember you enter that state of mind according to the amount of time that you spend running. The first twenty minutes consist of getting out all the physical and psychological quirks: both mind and body are protesting.

This is the time when you ask yourself, "What the hell am I doing here?" It's important to keep on going, however. Many people quit jogging because they never get out of that initial phase of discomfort and into the next—a sort of mild euphoria that generally hits around the twenty-minute mark.

After thirty minutes you should be safely into the "runner's high." At this point in running therapy there is generally a tremendous outburst of talking, the result of the "second wind"—a renewed energy and a relaxing of the brain's censoring device. Thoughts and feelings pour out uninhibited by the usual veneer of self-consciousness.

It's a good idea to carry a small pad with you to jot down important insights when you finish running. Or leave some time immediately after your workouts to sit and recollect your thoughts and put them into a special runner's journal. As we shall see, these notes will be the key to your interpretation of the unconscious material evoked in the inner-directed framework of the run.

After forty minutes you may notice changes in visual perception. Colors may seem brighter and more intense. Next you experience a certain distortion in body perceptions. You may feel as though you're floating—or as though you're not really running at all, but standing still. Or you may feel taller or more compact than you have before.

After an hour, you'll be in an altered state of consciousness similar to meditation, prayer, and some drug experiences and dreaming. Emotions may well up from some untapped source and tears may come unexpectedly with the resurrection of some childhood memories. "If you keep on going, you will begin to resonate with your unconscious," Kostrubala promises, "and the experience will be delightful." You'll know when you've reached this phase of the run, for you'll begin to fantasize and dreamlike images will float across the cinematic canvas of the mind.

In this stage, messages from the unconscious may also be triggered by cues in the outside environment and a complex of emotional associations may suddenly be evoked by something as simple as a seagull or a poplar tree. What follows is an instant recognition of the universal nature of the object, as though the thing were reunited through one's gaze with the world of forms and essences, the primal substate for the creation of all birds or all trees.

Kostrubala describes how he tapped into the archetypal unconscious just before the Honolulu Marathon in December, 1974. "I got up before dawn and ran toward Diamond Head, on a training run. Suddenly ahead of me was a tiny blonde girl with long straight hair, pushing her bike. It had a load of undelivered newspapers on the front handlebars in a gray bag. She was about six or seven. And her smile penetrated the murky depths of my memory and released all the loves, pleasures, kindnesses, tenderness, of all the women I have ever known. There was also in that little girl the interlocking of Mary, Eve, and Helen of Troy. All of these things came to my conscious attention." The little girl touched a chord in Kostrubala's unconscious that contained symbols of revered womanhood throughout the ages.

Dreams and Visions

The next surprise is that running enables you to conjure up inchoate images from the depth level of the psyche even as you sleep. Because joggers dream more vividly and more often, it's wise to keep a journal of those messages from the unconscious that come to you in dreams. Since running can give you an energy boost that will keep you going strong for several hours and interfere with sleep, it's best not to run late at night. Instead, schedule a series of early morning runs, and use your workouts to recollect the images and fantasies of your dreams.

Instead of bolting out of bed in the morning, set your alarm an extra ten minutes early. Rise slowly and ease yourself into your running gear. Don't talk to anyone on your way out, and try to stay in that semi-waking state between dreaming and fully focused consciousness.

The dream cycle grows in line with the basic physiological rhythms of the body. That may be why the longer we run, the more soundly we sleep and the deeper we dream. Furthermore the body sensations we collect in the daily run go into our "mind bank" and come back as the physical sensations of our dreams. So jogging is really a way of gathering material for the serial adventures of your sleep. If you suddenly stop running, don't be surprised if you have a restless night, then grow moody and begin to gain a little weight. A curtailment of the dreaming cycle will produce anxiety, irritability, and an increased appetite. Moreover, you won't be able to integrate the events of the day—your feelings about your work and reactions in personal relationships—with the rest of your personality structure.

Running will also evoke the tremendous healing power of your dreams and help you confront those "unacceptable" feelings you've repressed throughout the day.

When a twenty-four-year-old woman injured in an industrial accident came to Kostrubala for running therapy, she could barely walk. Her orthopedist and neurosurgeon could find no medical basis for her worsening condition and she complained of severe pains in her lower back. But after a program of stretching exercises and graduated running alongside Kostrubala, she began to recall her dreams, and through them eventually recognized that her back pains were symbolic of her fear and hatred of men. To avoid contact with them, she had "crippled" herself. In her dreams, her mother appeared as a hostile figure, warning her against involvement with the opposite sex. When the young woman saw how she had simply taken over her mother's anxieties she was able to dispel her unconscious resentments, and her crippling pains disappeared.

But running also activates dreams of epic significance, bringing messages of the collective mind that can aid us during major life transactions. These "big dreams" are instantly recognizable, for they also instill a sense of awe and have an immediate impact on the dreamer. If you are perplexed by a crisis in your work or personal relationships and don't know which direction your life is taking, go out for a leisurely run and let the answer come to you in your sleep.

While this may sound like a novel approach to psychological problem-solving, the early Greeks believed that during sleep the soul would return to the world of forms and essence to be educated and refreshed. And until the Middle Ages dreams were included in medical diagnoses as precognitions of the cure. More recently, Jung restored dreams to their ancient status as links with a larger collective mind. Now we have discovered that the *longer* we run, the more contact we may have with this universal or cosmic consciousness, and the more access we have to creative and spiritual symbolism in our dreams.

Harvey A was a vice-president of a large corporation at the age of twenty-seven, and the uncompromising, aggressive qualities that earned him his early business success soon disrupted his family life.

After his marriage failed, Harvey joined the Teacher Corps in New Mexico, and by his own account, spent most of his time "getting stoned in the cotton fields with the

Indians." After eight lonely months in the desert, he returned to the West Coast and started running. During this period of reevaluation of his life goals and his relationship with other people, Harvey was running six to ten miles a day, and had the following dream:

"I was walking down a country road with two friends, when suddenly one of them levitated and his body raised up into the sky. There appeared around him three fish in translucent pockets of liquid, one each suspended in red, yellow, and blue colored water. Then I saw a blue bust, covered with a shawl, which began to rotate in the sky. As it turned, I could tell it was a statue of the Virgin Mary, and as I looked at her, the Madonna came to life and smiled down at me. It was the most remarkable moment of grace. She was the eternal feminine, the mother earth— the side of myself that I'd been afraid of. I'd always looked outside of myself for solutions to my problems, but this came from within and seemed to mark the turning point of my life."

The dream is filled with symbols of religious affirmation (which the dreamer successfully borrowed from another tradition since he was not raised a Catholic). The three fish represent the trinity, or the unity of the ego, personal unconscious, and collective unconscious. The three men walking down the country road reinforce this, since one of them (the spiritual self) raises up to the heavens to be transformed, while the other two (the ego and the intellect) are the "spectators" who receive the blessing from the Madonna, a representative of the collective or universal mind. And as the dreamer himself recognized, the Virgin also embodies his feminine side and all the qualities he had neglected in favor of satisfying his male intentionality and driving ambition. The message from the unconscious is "It's all right to be gentle and understanding of yourself and other people. Furthermore, you will succeed by doing this."

In running, the body and mind are "entrained," or working together in such a way that they are both governed by the same dynamic laws. When we experience intense emotional stress and are in need of some prophetic answer to our problems, we carry a psychic charge with us into the run. There is a parallel buildup of physical energy which prompts the discharge of symbolism from the unconscious during dreams and which furthers the process of resolution. The runner, then, is like a miniature universe in the process of creation, spewing out dreams like stellar bodies whirling into psychic space.

Kostrubala recalls that his own most memorable dream occurred directly after running the Los Angeles Marathon. At the time he was searching for a creative way to express his feeling that running aroused the archetypal images necessary for psychic development. The fact that his dream occurred after a four-hour run also reinforces his theory that the degree to which we penetrate the collective mind and enter altered states of consciousness is directly proportionate to the time frame of the run.

"A large, black, shiny creature was standing at the edge of the sea. It was armless, but with a great tail—so strong it could rock its entire body back and forth. I had surprised it laying its eggs. When it tried to get back into the sea, the surface was dense, packed in, frozen. The creature dived, hit the water, and bounced off several times. Finally it summoned up all its power and energy and crashed through. I ran up to the eggs, which were bluish green and sticky, and gathered them into a large cooking pot. As I heated up the pot and stirred the eggs with a large stick, they turned into fifty small things—like crabs."

The dream took Kostrubala back in time to observe the

mysteries of evolution. The creature was his unconscious representation of our animal and prehuman ancestors; the black, frozen sea stood for the impenetrability of the collective unconscious, the dark side of the soul which communicates through primal symbols and whose images are often as strange to us as the ocean creature. As in the beginning of all life, the creature came out of the sea and onto land and gave birth to a new form of life. Its offspring were liberated from this primal chaos through Kostrubala's "stirring" efforts—and were symbolic of the runners he had nurtured to another level of awareness through jogging therapy. Shortly after this dream Kostrubala was able to refine his theory of Paleoanalytic Psychology—the idea that running leads us through the different stages in man's evolutionary development and also provides the key to the future transformations of the body, mind, and soul.

The Runner's Journal: The Key to Interpreting the Mysteries of the Unconscious Mind

While individual dreams and body sensations may be difficult to divine without a therapist, you can disentangle the rich symbolic undergrowth of the psyche, made more fertile by the run, with the aid of your runner's journal. Begin to add your dreams and any strong images that come into your mind during the run to the notebook of body sensations you started earlier (Chapter 2). Be sure to list these experiences in the order in which they occur, however—and not according to separate categories (i.e., a special section for dreams and another for body feelings).

It is far easier to decode these messages of the unconscious if you examine them in chronological order. Instead of singling out a particular dream or body sensation for interpretation, look at an entire sequence of both dreams and body feelings and you will be able to see the symbolic narrative that strings these psychic events together.

As I look back over my running journal and dream log I can see a record of my psychological progress with regard to certain recurring themes: body awareness, self-consciousness, and fear of competition. I've listed some of the dreams and images from a three-month period shortly after I started running. These seem to organize themselves into a statement of the problem and then suggest a possible solution—I've added explanatory notes (with the benefit of hindsight) in the right-hand column:

February 10, 1977
Body feeling while running: a loosening of the body. Feeling like a snake.

Initial phase of running. Body feelings identified with prehuman ancestors. Secure, flexible, powerful, body feelings.

March 5
Image while running: vision of endless falling, fear of losing balance as I run faster. Followed that night by a dream: I am sitting at the foot of my father's easy chair. The floor spreads and separates and I fall through into a bottomless black space.

Identification of primal fear in man: terror of falling. Recurring dream in childhood resurfaces. I realize I associate loss of physical control with fear of abandonment.

March 27
Dream: I watch a film of

Self-consciousness intrudes.

myself running fast and well, but know I haven't done it in real life yet.

I am also inhibited by my preconceived ideas of success.

April 8
Body feeling while running: I sense that I am "sitting on my legs" or "riding in the saddle" as I run.

(Common symptom of altered state of consciousness in the forty-to-sixty-minute range of the run.) For the first time, my body takes over, my mind "sits." A pleasant feeling.

April 15
Experience while running: the day before my first race, a four-miler. I keep stopping because I have pushed myself too hard in the beginning of the workout. And because I am afraid of "not being good enough," I want to quit. Also I know my strategy should be to start slow and pick up speed, but I am embarrassed by a creeping start.

Again, self-consciousness intrudes, the body clamps down. Fear of competition and "what other people will think." I got "sick" and didn't enter the race.

May 1
Dream: I am running, my legs swing in long wide arcs in front of me and I can feel my entire body

The unconscious is establishing a "success image" in my brain and giving me the message: pay attention stretching. Am completely absorbed in my body sensations and in how I am running. I round a corner and pick up speed and am told by a crowd at the end that I was actually in a race and I have WON!

to your own internal process, your unique body-feelings. *You* come first, the race is secondary. That's what "winning" really means.

The dream sequence begins with a primal sensation of power, of being wily and flexible, like a serpent in Eden. Then the inevitable fears ensue—of falling and abandonment, followed by another universal downfall—the unconscious acceptance of other people's standards. Yet the lessons of the run and the dynamics of my dreams focused my attention on my own unique physical and psychic processes.

It wasn't until I started running and keeping a journal of my dreams and imagery associations that I began to understand the conflict between what I *could* do and what I thought I *should* do. I had previously been too self-conscious and self-critical and, instead of letting my goals unfold naturally, had always pushed myself to achieve and then failed to appreciate my efforts or my ultimate success. Finally I learned to trust my own internal cues and stop worrying about what other people think—not just about my jogging, but the way I run my life.

At the same time I learned to let each run be formed from within; I also found it easier to pay attention to the nuances of my feelings with regard to work and personal relationships. And with this newfound self-acceptance I also managed a relaxed and respectable first race: the 7.8 mile San Francisco "Bay to Breakers" in sixty-seven minutes flat.

Decoding the Messages from the Dark Side of the Psyche

When we run, we activate a primitive, metaphorical way of looking at the world and revive the archetypes of the ancient, animistic religions, images with the power of the sun and the serpent, pagan gods like Pan, that are symbolic of the earth and regeneration. We are going back in time to images that were once invoked by priests and shamans, early practitioners of healing who knew that transformation did not occur on the intellectual plane but required a transference of physical and psychic energy. Combining religious symbols—to stimulate the unconscious—with the rhythmic and exhaustive movement of sacred dancing, they created a tension and finally a harmony of body and mind, similar to the unity we experience in the run. What these ancient "therapists" were doing was evoking the dark side of the psyche, that part of the unconscious that often makes us behave in ways contrary to our conscious wishes and desires.

Like the magic circle which protects the initiate from "harmful" forces during these pagan religious practices, running provides a stable and controlled testing ground for the elements of the unconscious to emerge. It also evokes a rich personal mythology, a tapestry of images and dreams—filled with ancient symbols of transformation—to aid us in our modern search for meaning.

During a self-imposed period of sexual abstinence a thirty-year-old divorcée was warned of the danger of sublimating her sexual needs when she became "possessed" by a mythic archetype at a particularly pastoral moment in her jog. "I was running rather slowly through the woods and kept wishing my body would pick up speed," she recalls. "Suddenly my hips began to move by themselves. I felt a surge of power in my loins, my torso seemed to grow heavier, thicker, more masculine, and almost saturnine. My God, I thought, I'm turning into Pan!"

While she thought she could ignore her own sexuality, she found that what she wished to repress still had the power to control her in the form of the ancient satyr and seductive forest god.

It is often through such mythical symbols that we come in contact with the dark side of the psyche and begin to reconcile those forces with the light of reason. Because the unconscious mind frequently seems to pull us in the opposite direction of our rational intention, Jung has referred to the relations between these dual aspects of the psyche as an "enantiodromia"—which means, literally, "running the other way." Running can help us reconcile these warring factions as it lowers our emotional resistances and brings these hidden feelings to the fore.

We can take a cue from primitive cultures like the Senoi, a Malaysian tribe who use their dreams to confront the dark side of the psyche and to liberate themselves from unpleasant and constricting anxieties that might spill over into their waking hours.

When a Senoi child has a frightening dream of falling, for example, he is told by his parents how to transform this negative dream experience into a positive one. "That's not a *bad* dream," they explain. When you have it again, simply let yourself enjoy the feeling of floating through space. Think of the air as soft and supportive and do not be afraid."

By the time the child does have the dream again, he has programmed himself not to be afraid of the falling sensation. He does not grow rigid and try to resist his terror with the tensed muscles of his body. Instead he allows himself to reexperience the situation without anxiety, in a calm and accepting manner, and his fearfulness disappears.

Because running reaches back to our primal core of being, we can combat man's oldest and most instinctive fears as they surface in our dreams. Robert Ardrey points out that the fear of falling dates back millions of years, perhaps even to the Miocene, when our ancestors slept in trees like monkeys and a twitch or turn would send the body plummeting to predators below. Recurring dreams of falling, then, may actually be remnants of our evolutionary past. Dreams of flying, on the other hand, may be genetically retained body sensations harkening back to prehistoric times when our forebears swung apelike through the trees.

Other common nightmares, originating deep in our primal past, include those dreams in which we are desperately trying to get away, running as hard and fast as we can to escape some real or imaginary monster. The Senoi also have a therapeutic way of dealing with this inborn "fight or flight" response and its manifestation in our dreams. Psychologist Patricia Garfield, who studied the Senoi attitudes toward dreaming, reports the following exchange:

A child explained that he had been chased by a tiger in his dreams; "I ran as fast as I could, but he kept getting closer and closer, my legs couldn't move any faster. And I woke up very frightened."

The boy's father counseled him not to run away but to confront and overpower this danger in his dreams.

"It was good you had that dream, son," he replied. "But you made a big mistake in it! Tigers you see in the jungle in the daytime can hurt you and you may need to run, but the tigers you see in your dream at night can only hurt you *if* you run away from them. They will continue to chase you only for as long as you are afraid of them. The next time you have this dream, and you will have it again soon —you must turn around and face the tiger. If it continues to attack you, you must attack it."

As we see from this illustration, the appropriateness of the "fight or flight" response is actually reversed in our dreams. In the daytime we can rid ourselves of tension and anxiety by running, but in our sleep we must not flee, but rather face those demons which pursue us and conquer the things we fear.

How can you use your dream power to attack the repressed contents of the psyche? If you have a nightmare or dream which disturbs you, identify the person or situation which you are running away from. Tell yourself that you will *not* run away again, but turn and attack your adversary and gain control of the situation. Go out for a run and, as you're jogging, review the imagery of your dream. Feel yourself becoming strong and indomitable. And imagine yourself turning around and conquering the threatening figure—whether it's a lover who tried to devour you in your dream, a mother suffocating you with her love, or a boss whose criticism you dreamed would ruin your career. Program yourself to take aggressive action in your dreams and to fight back, so as you subdue these figures in your dream you will actually be killing the fear you hold inside. Then, after you've slain these dragons of the unconscious, leave yourself with a peaceful thought: envision your enemy changing into a sympathetic figure with no wish to harm you. Picture yourself facing him openly, confidently, and without fear. Because you're more open to suggestion when you run than at any other time, you can feed this positive dream programming directly into your unconscious and thereby rid yourself of nagging fears that otherwise would stalk you in your dreams.

EIGHT

How to Meditate in Motion: Running As the Western Zen

William James once remarked that nature was the catalyst for the most striking examples he had found of religious revelation and ecstasy. And runners who meditate as they train may also reach this transcendental peak more than other athletes because they spend long periods in contemplation out of doors.

Like those who've turned to the inner game of tennis and the philosophies of the martial arts, aikido and T'ai Chi, no longer satisfied with the traditional separation of "mind" from physical pursuits, the "Zen" or meditative runner is a new breed of inner-directed athlete whose daily workout has the quality of religious ritual. Many of the 25 million joggers in the United States are running simply to lose weight, avoid heart attacks, or compete in road races, but those who run primarily for the spiritual high find the rhythmic pattern of the breath and heartbeat has a hypnotic effect, while increased oxygen to the brain is a stimulant for altered states of consciousness.

Like the early mystics, called "athletes of God" for their ability to fast and sit in meditation beyond the normal limits of endurance, the spiritual runner trains with the dedication and single-mindedness of a monk, testing his faith and perseverance, a pilgrim moving in a Dante-esque mind-space over solitary stretches of country road and urban landscapes, on a metaphysical journey of the soul. But there are many milestones on his route to heightened awareness having more to do with the time than the distance jogged. Even for the most accomplished, the first twenty minutes consist of general discomfort. But after half an hour, you've worked out the tension in your body and are beginning to be lulled by its rhythmic movement. This is the period when the "runner's high"—a sort of mild euphoria—sets in. After forty minutes, you lose the ability to organize your thoughts, and ideas flash in from the periphery of your inner vision. This is the problem-solving state where seemingly irrelevant musings pop out as answers to previously puzzling questions. Then after an hour, you're in an altered state of consciousness where visual perception changes and colors blend together—and mild hallucinations may occur. If you keep on going, you'll stumble into a state of "aesthetic arrest"—or what others refer to as the "Zen" experience—where the runner feels a mystical unity with his surroundings and is suspended in space and time like the figure immortalized in flight on Keats's Grecian urn.

"My early-morning runs are like prayer time," explains Sister Ann, a San Diego nun who petitioned her order for permission to run the mountain trails at Big Bear. "At first I felt so alone. When I got to the top of the mountain, I thought, 'No one on earth knows where I am!' Suddenly I realized God did. As I ran through the tall pines I *knew* his attention was on me." Like Sister Ann, most people who look upon their jogging as a spiritual as well as physical exercise are very different from the ordinary athlete. They shun competition, are less likely to be concerned with logging times and distances, and are more apt to describe their training in transcendental terms. "Unless you trip over a rock it's not the usual awareness," explains twenty-seven-year-old Phyllis Haynes, who started running as part of her karate training. "These are moments of pure joy." Now a black belt, Phyllis speaks of her daily stint of ten miles as Zen conditioning. "I often wonder how I got from point A to point B," she marvels, "because after a while my body's running *me*." And poet Roger Eischens writes in *Run to Reality:* "The more I run, the more I become like the monks and Zen fanatics and the Indians in knowing that I'm part of this earth and everything is transient. Running wipes away the cultural dust from our feeling of being, casting aside the trappings of a society alienated from the rhythms of nature, and which, in turn, alienates us from ourselves."

For these initiates, the marathon is not a race against time or other runners but a test of mental strength that holds the possibility for religious awakening and rebirth. In the last six miles as the body runs out of glycogen fuels, the runner undergoes a kind of physiological death that's been likened by some to passing through the Dark Night of the Soul. This is the time when your body is saying, "I can't" and your mind is saying, "I will." Even such cool professionals as Olympic gold medalist Frank Shorter admit that no one knows what's going to happen in the last six miles. "You don't know whether your mind is ready to put your body through it," says Shorter, who rails against any romanticizing of his training and adopts the strict asceticism of a saint. And according to psychologist Michael Murphy, when we run, we create and destroy two and a half million red blood cells per second, and at the same time, begin a parallel process of discarding and generating new thought forms. "Running, even in its gentlest approach," he says, "allows us to be reborn."

Though twenty-six miles has been the mythical bench-mark for psychological as well as physical heroism for more than twenty-five centuries of running, the experience of mystical rebirth may be more a function of the attitude of the athlete than the distance logged. At a certain level of proficiency we may impose this psychological framework on the run, regardless of its length. Hence, what we may actually be experiencing is the rebirth of the spiritual, at a major turning point in culture and in consciousness, when we have overestimated the powers of rational thought and found the purely intellectual lacking in subtlety and passion.

For Sri Chinmoy, who conducts weekly meditations at the United Nations in New York, running is but a prelude to spiritual awakening. The guru urges all his students to get in shape fast by jogging and to meditate while running as part of their spiritual training. Though he's not unsympathetic—"Losing weight is harder than realizing God," he smiles—he has admonished several of his disciples, "Look at you—you're fat and weak! Get out and run!" The former decathlon champion from northern India believes that running is a tool for personal growth leading from self-acceptance to self-transcendence.

Sri Chinmoy routinely organizes ten-mile "Love and Serve" runs to benefit the U.N. Childrens' Fund, and can be seen at six-thirty on the high school track every morning near his home in Jamaica, Queens, outstripping his most strapping disciples. "Run fast, faster, fastest to your spiritual goals!" he yells, sprinting briskly by. "When we run we meditate," he offers, "and when we meditate we're running on the inner plane."

The inner marathon of self-realization Sri Chinmoy speaks of is no idle boast. The guru has produced 122,000 paintings, written 360 books, 2,000 devotional songs, and once penned 843 poems in a single sitting. His idea is that the body must become the basis for one's spiritual endurance. In 1976, Sri Chinmoy's disciples ran 9,000 miles across the United States carrying a flaming "liberty torch" in celebration of the nation's bicentennial.

The Physiology of Meditation: The Biological Process of the Run

But what actually happens in this altered state that some runners take for granted—and that takes others by surprise? Like the mystic who casts off his usual perceptions of space and time in order to see more deeply into reality, the runner leaves behind objective measurements of these dimensions to rediscover his own biological clock and body space. As body temperature rises, a minute can be perceived as a period as brief as thirty-six seconds, while a three-hour marathon might seem, subjectively, to be as short as one hour and forty-eight minutes. Physical boundaries seem to alter, related to the pumping action of the heart and lungs. While most of us a little short on exercise tend to think of "I" as being centered somewhere in the chest or head, with each pulsing movement the runner's sense of self expands, pouring through the limbs into the toes and fingertips, filling the entire body like a viscous liquid.

The body is then the touchstone for awakening consciousness and the means by which we move from automatic responses to another state of mind. The function of the conscious brain is really the mundane one of limiting our sensory experience and selecting out only that information which is pertinent to survival. In *The Doors of Perception*, Aldous Huxley writes:

> Each one of us is potentially Mind at Large. But insofar as we are animals, our business is at all costs to survive.

To make biological survival possible, Mind at Large has to be funneled through the reducing valve of the brain and nervous system. What comes out at the other end is a measly trickle of the kind of consciousness which will help us stay alive on the surface of this particular planet.

Certain persons, however, seem to be born with a kind of bypass that circumvents the reducing valve. In others, temporary bypasses may be acquired either spontaneously, or as the result of deliberate "spiritual exercises."

Prolonged contemplation and repetitive physical activities both break the shell of habituation, allowing us to transcend the normal boundaries of our restrictive consciousness and see the world anew. Archery and the martial arts have long been taught as spiritual disciplines in the East and for centuries Buddhist monks have broken up their rounds of meditation with bursts of circle running in the inner courtyards of the monasteries. At the Rochester Zen Center, students are now beginning to take long runs before their Sunday meditation, and the Zen-do in Tassajara, California, last year held its first sixteen-mile "Noh-race" over mountain trails.

Mystics have long known that subjecting the body to unusual stress will bring about a restructuring of the psyche and a recrystallization of thought. Saint Jerome beat his breast with a rock and Buddha fasted for forty-nine days before he had his vision, each of these formidable exercises in asceticism. But long-distance runners are making a profound readjustment of this ancient wisdom, using healthful workouts to stretch beyond the ordinary limits of their senses. And as more runners discover altered states of consciousness, and a Zen condition where the body seems to run itself, students of TM and yoga are also finding that it's easier to meditate in motion and to quell the rebelliousness of the body with the repetitive rhythm of the run.

Why are we suddenly running from five to twenty-five miles in the service of enlightenment? While we desperately need the benefits of meditation—a breaking of our automatic responses and routines that allows us to resume our daily activities with a fresh mind and nourished spirit—most Westerners fear the inactivity and the emptiness of traditional Zen meditation. The confrontation of a blank wall and the space behind the mind is an alien and sometimes terrifying experience and instead of calming the nerves and bringing us gently to a state of relaxation, it often arouses sensations of physical disintegration and anomie. For those unable to sit still, running provides a "cooling-down" period. Moreover psychiatrist William Glasser has found that runners attain a certain addictive high during which they are able to drain off tensions and release negative emotions—yet they are able to ease into the meditative state, secure in the framework of the run, and knowing they have something else "to do." Glasser also discovered that runners become addicted to their transcendental states and find it easier to achieve them on a regular basis than those who opted for sedentary meditation.

It's not surprising that in the West, the meditative "way of action" is more popular than the contemplation of difficult philosophical riddles and koans, for we are already living far too much in our heads, unable to make contact with the rest of our bodies, at the same time feeling compelled to fill our schedules to the brim in search of the one activity that will bring us "inner peace." Maybe, we think, if we keep on running from one thing to another, we will find it. But the metaphor is particularly apt, for the possibility for redemption lies within what we perceive to be our tragic flaw: we can become centered in the midst of our activity and use the motion of the body to calm the ceaseless stirrings of the mind.

The directions for being in the inner spaces of the mind are actually the same as those for classic Zen meditation. When we run, we focus on the posture and the breath. We place our body and mind in right order, concentrate on the flow of "being" in our running, and count our steps as a sitting monk might count his breaths. Suddenly the simplest things are the most important. As we leave behind the fierceness and the competition and our daily striving for perfection to discover a moment of being "without self-criticism and judgment, we stop our "doing" and simply learn to "be."

End-Watching vs. Beginner's Mind

In running, as in Zen, we face a wedge of boredom, a chunk of empty time that separates our usual compulsive thinking from a state of altered awareness. In this interface, we simply watch the movement of our thoughts across the proscenium of consciousness, without exerting judgment or choice; at the same time, we allow the body to find a rhythm of its own, and let the action of the run be formed from *within*.

Preoccupation with goals often interferes with our ability to let the body flow and to experience "empty time." Dr. David Shainberg, a New York psychiatrist, calls this phenomenon "end-watching" and describes it as a building anxiety near the end of the run related to a sense of encroaching time.

If the jogger stops focusing on the step-by-step progress of the run and allows himself to think where he should be in the next few minutes of the run, or how hard it's going to be to get there, suddenly his legs get heavier, his breath shorter, and what started out as enjoyment suddenly looms up an as impossibility. Shainberg has identified those who have this problem as high achievers, goal-oriented individuals who overemphasize the rational as opposed to the feeling side of their personalities. With such a definition, there's a good chance that "end-watching" afflicts the majority of joggers, for demographic surveys show that most long-distance runners in the United States have high yearly incomes and work in high-pressure professions requiring graduate degrees. The Zen of running requires an intuitive approach, however, and an attitude that is essentially nonjudgmental and trusting, one of "I don't know what I'm going to do, but I have complete faith in my ability to do it."

Shainberg describes his own battle with end-watching in the run: "The longer the run, the sooner it appears. I set my mind on the end of the run. It may be no more than the top of a hill, beyond which I cannot see, but it becomes a mechanical fixation. Or it may be the image of being finished and out of the agony of having to breathe with the rhythm of the run. About two miles from my goal I am already thinking 'Can I make it?' If I don't make it, what then? Am I asking can I make it to my own death? It seems such a silly question. Of course I will make it to that goal. Everybody does. Am I asking can I make it to my death 'perfectly' or 'successfully'? This absurdity makes me laugh. On my tombstone they will put: Here lies David Shainberg. He was perfect and successful in getting here.

"As I run on, a wave of relaxation comes over me. I don't have to push myself. I can stop whenever I feel like stopping. But then there is a doubt. If I do not set up these efforts, these arbitrary pushes, will I ever get to any of my goals? I am afraid nothing will happen to me, that I will lose touch with reality, which at this moment seems to need to be grabbed, rather than depended on, to support me. When the momentum comes again and I am back with my legs in the rhythm of the run, I see I have lived a kind of death, as I gave up my thoughts of 'I' and 'me' and ceased to want everything to be easy at every moment."

Yet there are some times when everything is right from the very beginning, when we are able to lock into what Zen master Shunryu Suzuki called "beginner's mind"—a state of no expectations, without judgment and choice.

"Every mile I run is my first," explains George Sheehan, a New Jersey cardiologist in his fifties who's been writing on the mental and physical healing aspects of running for over fifteen years. "Every day I put on my running clothes I am born again. Every hour on the road, a new beginning. Seeing things as if for the first time, seeing the familiar as unfamiliar, the common as uncommon. Doing what Goethe said was the hardest thing of all—seeing with my own eyes that which is spread before me. Bringing to that running, that play, the attitude of a child, the perception of a poet. Being a beginner with a beginner's mind, a beginner's heart, and a beginner's body.

"There is no other way to run. No other way to live. Otherwise my runs become dull, uninspired interludes—a routine part of the humdrum apathy and indifference which the poet John Wheelock called a shield between us and reality. It becomes a chore, a habit. And habit kills awareness and separates us from ourselves. Each day I rediscover how to breathe, taste the air, and feel it move through my lungs. I learn to exhale totally and groan and grunt, marking my passage through the fields and trees like some animal.

"It is relatively easy to return to the basics with the body. But to have a beginner's mind and heart is a different matter. I think of the good things that happened in my beginning. When I was not afraid to respond to my feelings. Before I was taught not to cry. Before I learned that humor had a time and a place and deep emotions had best be concealed, that passion be left unfelt. When I run, I go back to those better days. Now no emotion is foreign to me. I express myself totally. My body and heart and mind interact and open me to the infinite possibilities only a beginner can envision."

How to Reach the Meditative State

Not everyone reaches this trancelike state during which Tibetan monks are reported to run for twenty-four hours without stopping, and Western devotees are apt to fall in love with other joggers, or sense ancestral ties to cavemen loping through primeval forests. But not everyone who runs is seeking a new way to meditate or a new metaphysics.

Those who treat the body as a machine may be likely to expect nirvana after plodding through ten miles because they have met the physical requirements: now where is their psychological reward? If you want mechanical fitness, follow the charts that tell you how far to push pulse and how fast to run in fourteen minutes for maximum cardiac massage. If, on the other hand, you want to experiment with a new way of being, try running with a soulmate, and let the movement of your life unfold in the rhythm of the run.

If you find it difficult to focus your attention, there are some simple meditations you can use to bring yourself back into the step-by-step of the run. One is simple breath counting, from one to four and back again. (If you only count from one to four, you won't have to worry about missing a breath and you won't begin to panic when you reach your thousandth one, thinking that you'd better quit, because you've got to be exhausted by now.)

The "Safe Harbor" meditation is particularly helpful over difficult stretches and can be used to avoid the end-watching game in the last segment of the run. Imagine yourself anywhere in the world that you feel peaceful and protected. Run with your eyes half closed and picture yourself in these surroundings. Or tell yourself over and again, "I am coming home." Think of all the people that you love running close beside you, or meeting you with encouragement at different points along the way.

Try the Tibetan log meditation on days when you're besieged by nagging, unpleasant thoughts after a hard day's work, or are having difficulty just clearing your mind. Think of yourself running alongside a long and powerful river, and picture several logs floating downstream. Each time you have a vexing thought, attach it to a log and follow it, in your mind's eye, to a point where the river meets a deep and fathomless gorge, and the log is pitched out and over the falls.

The Way of the Body: Running and Sensory Awareness Meditation

There are other, more sensual meditations that take us away from the mind-set of competition and into the inner-spaces of the self.

No more training logs. No more treating the body like a sophisticated machine. "The coach of the future will be an artist of the soul, a shaman, one who unhooks the soul where it is stuck," says Dyveke Spino, an innovative track coach and director of New Dimensions in Lifestyle, a firm which designs fitness programs for business and industry. The daughter of a Danish surgeon and an opera singer who socialized in Jack London's circle and danced with Isadora

Duncan, Dyveke is an ageless woman in her early forties with fine, strong limbs and an elfin face set off by a crop of impishly tossed hay-colored hair. Her eyes are deep-set, reflecting her chameleonlike disposition and an ever-changing sensitivity to her environment. A concert pianist and psychologist, Dyveke has been a ski instructor, taught "Tennis Flow" at Esalen, and started a storefront community school in the inner city. Now she teaches an innovative combination of flexibility exercises and running gaits and sensory awareness meditation. And, in an effort to take the pain out of practice, the boredom out of workouts, she provides a sensuous alternative to the old male system of grinding out the miles at an injury-prone aggressive pace. Dyveke herself proves a lyrical counterpoint of discipline and spontaneity, of masculine technique and fluid feminine response as she runs up Mount Tamalpais at dawn. "If I don't run that mountain every day," she laughs, "I'm not good for anything!"

At her seminars, nonathletes and former track stars alike are lulled into a relaxed running form with a series of sensory awareness meditations. (If you want to sample one, try reading this into a tape recorder. Use your most soothing voice, and speak slowly and gently, as though talking to a child. Get on all your gear, sit quietly for about ten minutes, and then listen.)

"Lie down on your back and stretch out your arms and legs. Align your body so you're perfectly balanced, your hips over your knees, your knees over your feet. Now imagine all the cells of your body starting to expand and open up. Picture a sunstar about six inches above your head, and feel this whirl of light come down into your forehead and down into your neck. Feel the white light streaming down your shoulders and pouring out the ends of your fingers. As it flows through your body, through your arms and legs, be aware of any place that's stiff or rigid, any imbalance between the right and left sides of the body, and send the light there.

"As it courses through your body, out through the bottom of your feet, you can feel the white light washing out all the agitation, all the debris, the blocked-up frustrations, all the undone deeds. You begin to feel light and refreshed, almost as if you were floating in a lighted flesh vehicle.

"You have your own energy body—of radiant, pulsing light. It is your own force field, blending with the things around you. Imagine yourself being lifted off the ground in this energy body. Merging with a pool of water. A cloud. And a tree. You can feel the bark of the tree as if it were your own skin. Your back as if it were the spine of the tree. Feel your hair blow like the leaves.

"You can run as though you don't even own a physical body. As though you were just a leaf, blowing effortlessly over the grass. Your joints and muscles are completely balanced and aligned, your psyche opened up and connected with all living things."

Dyveke's voice is deep, hypnotic. It echoes in the wood-hewn dining room of the Westerbeke Ranch, a hundred-acre spread south of the Napa Valley. The "earth mother" of distance running, Dyveke provides a welcome contrast to the strict "no-nonsense" approach of most male coaches. And the meditations she employs are far from the ascetic monotones of Zen. After the sensory awareness meditation, Dyveke leads students over horse trails, past a herd of bulls, and up a gentle hill to practice different running gaits, to trot and prance like animals in the open field. She tells them to imagine their "energy bodies" are condensed and to run in circles, blending and bouncing off one another like atoms in a free-form Brownian movement. This is a playful run, followed by sybaritic hot tubs and massage, and capped with a primitive ritual "snake dance." Twenty-five people join hands and begin to move slowly, spontaneously, to the quiet slapping of African drums that increase, imperceptibly, like the distance of the run, and rise to a full, hard thunder. With the sensuous streaming of the blood awakened by the running and the dance, the brain surrenders its routine consciousness, anxieties are devoured by the open-mouthed drums, leaving body and mind transformed.

NINE

Spiritual Athletes: The New Elite

"Sometimes I feel as if I'm out of my body altogether," says therapist Ted Smith, director of New York's Central Counseling Service. "Other times, when I run, I'm absorbed in Nature, or I have no memory of the distance that I've covered."

Distance runners aren't the only ones reporting out-of-body experiences and altered states: some athletes have even witnessed paranormal occurrences in professional sports.

In *The Ultimate Athlete,* George Leonard tells us that quarterback John Brodie, of the San Francisco Forty-Niners, experiences a "clarity of vision" where everything appears to move in slow motion. His intuition tells him where his pass is going to go, and on occasion, Brodie wills it out of the hands of the opposition and foils the attempted intercept. Dave Meggesey, former outside linebacker for the St. Louis Cardinals, confessed to Leonard that he was able to see auras around the players and could tell what the other team was going to do before they began to move. And aikido master Morei Uyeshiba was even able to change size and shape at will: on film he seemed to "disappear" from the hands of his attacker and materialize a few frames later, standing gracefully at the edge of the mat. If professional athletes have experienced an expansion of their psychic powers as a result of hard physical training, can many of the 25 million runners who train alone or use this time for meditation be evolving into a new psychological and physical elite?

The Simultaneous Transformation of the Body and the Mind

"A person with a high degree of cell fitness and mind development will have an unconscious reaction to every situation superior to one who is not as physically and intellectually well-endowed," wrote "the mystic renegade," Percy Cerutty, a seventy-eight-year-old Australian track coach, who produced such great milers as Herb Elliot and John Landy. Before a major competition, Cerutty gave his runners secret readings on the origin of the universe and man's place in the evolution of the species. He kept them secluded until moments before the actual event, and while his protégés warmed up near the stadium, Cerutty performed the ritual of running himself to exhaustion. "You might run faster today," he would gasp as he finished, "but you won't run any harder!"

What Cerutty discovered about the simultaneous transformation of the body and the mind from training Olympic athletes, psychologist Michael Murphy found in meditation at the Aurobindo ashram in Pondicherry, India. Unlike Eastern ascetics who claim the body is an aspect of our lower nature, Aurobindo taught that the spirit can directly "re-own" the body and through various siddhis, or shocks of energy, push the individual to a higher plane of consciousness. His theory is a sort of quantum mechanics of the soul, whereby greater mental powers are accompanied by increased strength and endurance, or induced by a sudden, intense physical *gestalt*.

Murphy returned from India to merge the formality of Eastern meditation with the dynamic energy of the West and to found Esalen at Big Sur, which has been the breakfront for new frontiers in altered states since 1962. He is presently investigating spiritual transformations and their analogs in sport, comparing distance runners in anaerobic states with yogis, buried alive, who survive with little or no oxygen, and the meditative trance of the Lung Gom Pa, Tibetan monks who run for twenty-four hours over rugged mountain trails, with the endurance of world class marathoners who maintain close to a five-minute pace per mile.

Obsessed with the vision of the body and the mind transcending present evolutionary limits, Murphy found former college distance champion Mike Spino (then married to Dyveke) to put his theories into practice. With Murphy's light frame and deft concentration, he was soon running close to a five-minute mile, at the age of forty-four, while Spino at twenty-nine was having "peak" experiences as he ran.

One day Spino went out to time himself on a six-mile course over a dirt and asphalt road, paced by friends in an automobile. It was raining. Cars were honking. But Spino ran the first mile comfortably in four and half minutes, "as if carried by a huge momentum." Then, feeling no weight or resistance, he "ran like a skeleton, as if the flesh had been blown off his bones," and finished the full six miles at the same four-and-a-half-minute pace. He sat down by the side of the road and wept, for he no longer knew who he was. Was he Mike Spino? Or "the one who had been running"?

In his book, *Beyond Jogging: The Innerspaces of Running,* Spino explains, "What I do cannot be termed jogging.

It is a way of running to evoke a spirit and a sense of possibility. Once I voyaged from remembering the sounds and smells of my grandfather's house to a feeling of watching my body from a place above itself. I often run from the Saint Francis Yacht Harbor, skirting the waterfront, out to the Golden Gate Bridge. Halfway into the four miles I stop at a precipice overlooking the sea and look for omens. What vessel in the sea, what ocean color, what tide will show the day's meaning? It is a run I could do a thousand times without repeating the experience. By varying my gait and speed, lightening or increasing my tempo, I change my metabolism and shift my mood. Sometimes I become speechless, and often at dusk, the run brings tears to my eyes."

After coaching Murphy (who soon set the record for his age division at the West Coast AAU championships), Spino went to work designing the Esalen running program, incorporating heavy doses of interval and resistance training. His goal: to orchestrate those physical breakthroughs which stimulate altered states of consciousness. Now those who lack the incentive to push beyond their present capabilities, or who don't even want to compete, may soon begin to crave the mental exhilaration of intense anaerobic workouts, once they find there's more to running than putting in the distance, at the same slow, steady pace.

The Esalen Training Program: A Variety of Tempos and Gaits

Most people subscribe to a program of endurance training, jogging for a long time at an even gait. But sooner or later they get bored or feel distressed that they're not getting any better. "If you keep on using the same metabolism," Spino cautions, "you'll approach your maximum level of fitness and then cease to improve. Not only that, but you'll miss the kinesthetic pleasure of running variations—and the joy of different movements!"

To bring you closer to your optimum physical condition —the prerequisite for heightened psychic powers—Spino has whipped up a training regimen that combines interval training and running tempos developed by Hungarian coach Mihaly Igloi, and animal gaits borrowed from the Australian Cerutty. These exercises are the beginning of a system of mind-body training which will eventually lead you deeper into the innerspaces of the run.

First you have to know your terms:

The Shuffle: This is basically a slow jog for warming up or moving slowly over long distances. Push out from the knees and take short steps, and carry one arm across the body in front of the belly. Move at less than 20 percent of your potential effort, and keep your foot-plant far back on the heel.

Fresh Swing: Increase your tempo to 20 to 40 percent of your maximum effort. Lift from the knee and you'll get a rolling movement from heel to toe.

Good Swing: This is the same motion as fresh swing but increased to 40 to 60 percent of your maximum effort. Beyond 80 percent, you'll be sprinting.

The Surge: This is logically a lunging forward, using your arms to propel you, while at the same time making a noise in the back of the throat that releases body tension and enables you to exert more strength. Make an exaggerated pumping motion with your arms, and then make the high-pitched sound, "Ping!" in your epiglottis, and you will get an added energy "surge."

The Shake-Up: This one is a free-form movement, arms loose and swinging, almost flopping from side to side. Imagine yourself as a large rag doll. Alternate your tempo and your foot-plant from a series of slow and large loping steps to fast, short, and choppy ones. Throw in a few shoulder shrugs to loosen up the muscles and relax the upper body.

After you've learned to play with these tempos, and you've discovered your own variations in gait and speed, Spino prescribes a series of training intervals tailored specifically to your body type, age, general fitness, and athletic ability. The average mesomorphic male, at age twenty-five, would be given a series of workouts completely different from an endomorphic female at thirty-seven, but to give you an idea of day one in *her* six-week fitness regimen, she would go down to the high school track oval, and after warming up (see Chapter 2) she'd do:

two minutes—shuffle
three 50-yard "shake-ups"
25 high knee lifts
two minutes—runs on spot
two minutes—shuffle/walk
two 60-yard fresh swing
two 60-yard—40-yard fresh swing and 20-yard surge
two 60-yard "shake-ups"

Spino can usually be found mid-field, standing at the edge of the pack of runners shouting out directions like a short-order cook. "Okay, Steve, four hundred-yard shake-ups, followed by three fifty-yard sprints. Betty, you try three fifty-yard shake-ups, then take fresh swing for five times sixty yards."

In his book *Running Home,* Spino gives a complex table of training programs for every level of fitness and body type, explaining each workout in a forty-two-day period with computerlike precision. Basically he has constructed a six-week training program, with five workouts per week, geared toward a final goal of running the mile in less than seven and a half minutes. His formula for each fitness level is the same, consisting of:

65 percent endurance training—long slow distance runs two or three times a week.

25 percent speed and tempo training—workouts based on the faster gaits, moving from the warm-up shuffle into fresh swing, good speed, then into surge and sprint form.

10 percent resistance training—running uphill or up flights of stairs. (Knee lifts can be substituted for rank beginners with undeveloped thigh muscles.)

The program can be distilled as follows:

The first two weeks: This is a time for building up endurance and getting a sense of the fluidity of your movement. Take three long slow distance runs a week. If you're just starting out, this may mean twelve minutes of combined walking and shuffle gait, easing up to eighteen minutes of the same. If you're more advanced and can run for a half hour comfortably, start out with five minutes of the shuffle and continue for twenty-five minutes in fresh swing. If you're already running for an hour at a time, take one shorter forty-five-minute workout and make the other two a full sixty minutes, also beginning with the shuffle, but easing into fresh swing and ending with good swing.

Don't strain yourself, but get your body used to the amount of effort needed for the various gaits and tempos. Spend another two days per week doing thirty-minute combinations of intervals, from shuffle through good swing, and including surge and sprint form. Always wind down with five minutes of shake-ups and allow yourself plenty of time to rest in between faster gaits. As you progress, you'll be able to increase your tempo and recover in a short time.

Forget resistance work or uphill training for the moment and spend most of your time on flat roads or smooth track ovals, running at a moderate pace.

The second two-week period: Now you'll begin to increase the amount of time you spend running intervals, cutting back your slow long-distance runs to two days of the week and adding another day of tempo training. You'll also start running up hills (at a 30-degree incline) or flights of stairs. Beginning joggers will do three flights, intermediates five flights, and advanced, seven, but you will only have to inflict this torture on yourself once a week.

Learn to gauge the amount of rest you need to recover from these workouts and always allow yourself to rest sufficiently before resistance training and the more strenuous interval workouts. You can keep up your long slow distance running, however, on those days you don't feel fresh, without fear of overstressing yourself.

The third two-week period: In the first week, you'll build yourself up with three long slow distance runs and cut back to only two days of interval training. Then the last week, you'll drop back to one distance run at the beginning of the week, and add three days of brief interval training, throw in one resistance workout, and rest for one day before you run the timed mile.

Spino's training method brings fast improvements to a variety of athletic talents. Graduates of the six-week program include Tommy, a forty-four-year-old Boston bartender who started out with a bit of a girth; Bruce, a twenty-nine-year-old featherweight, who renovates Victorian houses; Steve, a thirty-five-year-old management consultant, and Sylvia, a former airline stewardess who began jogging to lose weight. After six months of moderate training— running three times a week—they each ran a mile in less than 7:30—with Bruce coming in at a fast 5:02 pace.

At the same time you're making physical progress, however, Spino will lead you through a series of meditations designed to take your consciousness out of your body and enable you to run for long periods of time in a transcendental state.

The Esalen Meditation and Mental Imagery Program

First, Spino gives his runners visualizations to combat sluggishness and fatigue. He suggests you picture a large sky hook that pulls you off the ground with every step, or imagine a Brobdingnagian hand that swoops down and pushes you from behind. Then think of clouds beneath your feet. And if the day is hot and humid, imagine being sprayed with fresh, clear water from a spring or waterfall.

Next, he focuses on more sophisticated meditations concerning body density which will enable you to feel lighter and heavier at will. You can record his directions on a tape, stretched and relaxed out on the floor, and go through these exercises just before you run.

"Close your eyes and take a deep breath into your abdomen. Feel it extend, then exhale. Let all the muscles of your face relax. Now picture a valve in the side of your neck and draw a very heavy oily substance into your body with every breath. First it covers the part of your body that's touching the ground. Next it fills your shoulders, then the top of your back. Allow yourself to get as full as you can be.

"Now let the fluid seep out of your body. And with the fluid, release some tension, some anxiety, some emotional turmoil. Each time you breathe out, let go of something else.

"Think of the valve again—only this time fill yourself up with a substance lighter than air. It might be helium, or spun cotton. Make your insides like a bird's. This is the place we manufacture energy and internal light. You're lighter now than you've ever imagined yourself to be. Now open your eyes and try to transfer this awareness to your running."

You can also learn to draw added strength and endurance from a special "guide." Imagine that somewhere in the center of your being you carry the image of the "perfect runner." Deep within your being there is a place of stillness, an eternal quiet, a place of forms and essences that holds your ideal of perfect beauty. As you focus on this stillness and this peaceful inner place, the form begins to move and then to run effortlessly over hills and through long lush meadows. Follow this figure in your mind's eye —and imagine yourself running along with it side by side, as you match each other stride for stride.

With this image clearly in your mind, you will slowly rise and begin to walk with your eyes half closed. Everything on the periphery of your vision will be in soft focus, and you will retain in the center of your gaze the inward image of your perfect running companion. Today this messenger from the center of your being will lead you to our natural running style. As you run together, imagine you are *in* your perfect runner's body. Feel your arms and legs lifting, beginning to take on a new ease of form of their own. Think of the two of you merging in the same form. Imagine the mixing of your heartbeats. Feel his breath upon your breath. You are totally and completely in step, sharing the same reservoirs of strength and the same deep well of endurance. Run as long as you can carry this in mind.

The pursuit of distance running essentially requires you to control the nagging sensations of the body, from tightened muscles to tired knees, to ignore subjective feelings of heaviness and fatigue, and to banish those whimsical annoyances, from an itching elbow to a twitching nose, that interfere with an even pace and an easy running rhythm. It's almost as if we had a built-in mechanism for self-distraction that we have to learn to defuse before we can even approach our true potential in the run. Yet astoundingly, we can use visualization exercises which take the consciousness *out of the body*—and by projecting the mind to another place, we no longer have to wrestle with our petty internal growlings and complaints. A particularly valuable technique for runners is to imagine carrying your awareness just outside of your body—in a "witness self"—a special observer who travels with you as you run and watches your movements from a place about a foot above your head. Think of this "witness self" as a part of you, and as a sort of spare spiritual body you can repair to whenever your body begins to "act out" and draw your energy and attention away from the run.

Those of you who have practiced meditation will recognize this exercise as an extension of "watching your thoughts" (as in the Tibetan log meditation of the previous chapter). As we allow ourselves this objective distance from the workings of the mind, we are no longer pained by our petty attachments, hostilities, and griefs, but can see these things as part of the fluid nature of our humanity, passing across the screen of our inner vision. In the same way, the "witness" self is a projection of our higher self out of the body, enabling us to observe our minor physical pains and body feeling in much the same manner.

Murphy and Spino believe we are at this unique stage in human evolution where the training and meditation techniques of inner-directed running can make astounding endurance feats and shifts in consciousness accessible to large numbers of people. Yet while we're just beginning to explore meditations that can release powerful psychic forces and alter the visceral responses of the athletes, the Russians have been programming their athletes for Olympic competition using similar techniques for years. However, they're far from achieving the desired results of running as a comprehensive program of self-expansion and personal growth. Without this inner orientation, runners from the Eastern block countries have unfortunately been so mechanically "trained," they then are often unable to get out of the altered states they've entered for the purposes of competition. When Polish athlete Waldemar Cierpinski won the Olympic Marathon in 1976, he rested for an hour, then began circling the field in what everyone took to be another victory lap. The truth was he couldn't stop running!

TEN

The Road to Health: How Running Fosters Psychic Healing

In the meditative aspects of the run, we learn to be with all of ourselves, the good and the bad, without judgment, self-criticism, negative thoughts and fears. We focus on our heartbeat and our breath, we become aware of the process of life itself, of the basic syntax of all living things, and intuit our part in Nature's overall design. And in so doing, we activate the natural self-healing properties of the body and the mind.

Increasing Your Receptivity to Healing Thoughts

When we're in this meditative state we can effect dramatic changes in our bodies and promote our total health and well-being through use of some very simple guided imagery techniques. Biofeedback researchers have shown that we can send messages to the body and learn to control our breathing, heart rate, blood pressure, and skin temperature. Though we can't consciously command these changes, we can communicate with our inner psychological state in a special *symbolic* language—by creating mental images of the way we wish our bodies to respond. One young woman was able to control her dangerously irregular heartbeat by picturing a little girl on a swing, moving rhythmically to and fro, as she meditated sitting still. Now as we run we can increase our body's receptivity to these mental visualizations and also establish a finely tuned system of monitoring our physiological response.

Running and Meditation: Radical Adjunct Cancer Therapy

In 1971, cancer researcher Dr. Carl Simonton of Fort Worth, Texas, began to apply mental imagery techniques as an adjunct therapy to "incurable" cancer patients. Simonton's first test subject began to envision his cancer cells receding, being flushed out by the strong cells in his body, and crushed out of existence by the power of his cobalt treatments. Today he is alive and well beyond all medical expectation.

But Simonton noticed a marked difference in mental attitude between this patient and those who didn't get well. The others felt overwhelmed by the disease and literally couldn't picture themselves getting rid of it. They thought of their bodies as "the enemy" and so mentally worked against any medical efforts for a cure. These feelings of hopelessness were accompanied by a physical helplessness long before the disease reached epic proportions.

Like heart disease, cancer is the product of an affluent and sedentary society and is more likely to occur in the "well-to-do and indolent" than in the "poor and overworked." The highest number of cancer deaths fall to those in professions that involve the *least muscular effort*.

When Jack Scaff began taking cardiac patients to run marathons in 1975, Simonton saw how effective running had been with heart patients and thought he would try this radical approach to alternative cancer therapy. The idea that exercise would stem the course of malignancy was already strongly indicated by animal studies, and there is evidence, too, that exercise can stimulate the body's natural defense mechanism. In addition, Dr. Hans Selye, the Canadian biochemist, had suggested that exercise may have a beneficial effect on cancer patients by providing a channel for the release of tensions and stress.

Most striking was Simonton's discovery that the patients who outlived their predicted life expectancies had experienced the same kind of psychological changes that had been attributed to a regular running program. "The overall picture was that exercise could account for improved self-acceptance, less tendency to blame others, and less depression . . . and in general could be identified with the favorable prognosis for malignancy."

Simonton started his patients on a walk-run-jog program for one hour three times a week combined with mental imagery exercises. Perhaps the most impressive progress was made by a patient, a consulting staff psychologist at Simonton's Center for Cancer Counseling and Research, who completed the Honolulu Marathon with lung metastasis but experienced no breathing problems. "He even went out to dinner afterward while the rest of us fell asleep," Simonton reports. "To our knowledge this is the first time anyone with advanced cancer has completed a marathon."

A General Healing Meditation

If visualization and running can help bring about dramatic remissions and aid cancer cures, think what it can do for your own physical problems. I've adapted Dr. Simonton's mental imagery exercises for use as part of your daily workouts. So for whatever ails you—whether it's a stiffness in the neck and upper back, a minor bruise or local infection—you can give his "healing" meditation a try.

1. Before you go out to run, sit quietly in a comfortable chair in a dimly lit room and begin to draw your consciousness inward. Relax for a few minutes and separate yourself from the visual tensions and responsibilities of your day, then get up and slowly ease into the run.

2. As you jog, be aware of your breathing.

3. Take in a few deep breaths, and as you let out each breath, mentally say the word "Relax."

4. Concentrate on your face and feel any tension in the muscles of your face and around your eyes. Make a mental picture of this tension—it might be a rope tied in a knot or a clenched fist—and then mentally picture it relaxing and becoming comfortable, like limp rubber bands.

5. Experience the muscles of your face and eyes becoming relaxed. As they relax, feel a wave of relaxation spreading through your body.

6. Tense the muscles of your face and around your eyes, squeezing tightly, then relax them and feel the relaxation spreading through your body.

7. Move slowly down your body—jaw, neck, shoulders, back, upper and lower arms, hands, chest, abdomen, thighs, calves, ankles, feet—until every part of your body is more relaxed. For each part of the body, mentally picture the tension, then picture the tension melting away, allowing relaxation.

8. Now picture yourself in pleasant, natural surroundings—wherever feels comfortable for you. Mentally fill in the details of color, sound, texture.

9. Continue to picture yourself in a very relaxed state in this natural place for several minutes.

10. Now create a mental picture of any physical tension, tightness, or ailment that you suffer, visualizing it in a form

that makes sense to you.

11. Then picture your body's natural defenses and natural processes eliminating the source of the ailment or pain.

12. Imagine yourself healthy and free of the ailment or pain.

(If, for example, you have lower back pain, imagine your back uncoiling like a serpent, becoming straight and transforming into a long, golden staff. Think of rays of golden energy coursing up and down your spine and spreading throughout your entire body.

Then imagine yourself going through your daily routine without the back pain, feeling as strong and vibrant as you do now.

If you have stiffness or soreness around the joints, imagine little granules on the surface of your skin, working their way down in the joints, and massaging and cleansing out these areas. Then see yourself running, doing anything else you like to do, free of joint pain.)

13. See yourself proceeding successfully toward meeting your goals in life. Again, use any positive image that seems natural to you. It's important to make this final association between the eradication of your problem and the ability to proceed with the rest of your life goals. (If, for example, your goal is to run faster and farther, without cramping up or getting knee pains, picture yourself fluidly running the marathon. See yourself successfully completing it, coming to the finish line full of energy and in perfect, glowing health.

You can also envision sending a white light to any aching parts of your body as you run. Feel body tensions flowing out through exaggerated pores, or imagine a river of anxiety flowing out as you perspire.)

14. Use your running time to visualize your "perfect body

form," not just the "perfect runner" we described earlier, but the full you as a perfectly healthy and content human being. If you're emotionally distraught you can also use running as a form of psychic self-healing. As you run, picture your inner self as a lotus flower. Open up each and every petal, with positive thought about yourself or another person whom you love. As you unfold another petal, think of a friend, a relative whom you cherish, and as you let the gentle weight of all your loves and affections pull down every petal, think of as many loved ones as you can and try to stay in a calm, self-accepting state throughout your entire run as you watch your inner lotus bloom.

Healing Ourselves As We Heal Others

We can also affect our own health when we take others with us into the inner-consciousness of the run. When Dyveke Spino's friend, John, a thirty-eight-year-old IBM executive, was seriously injured in a motorcycle accident, she decided to meditate on his recovery with a distance run and swim, despite the fact that she had a stomach disorder and her right foot was swollen with a lymph infection.

As she eased her body into the pounding surf, she observed, "I felt totally relaxed, completely warm, as stroke after stroke I pulled against the undulating massive power of the choppy ocean," she recalls. "Soon I was more than a half a mile out to sea—much farther than I intended to be. I felt the rocking, rolling motion of the sea against my body. And with each stroke I took, the sunlight pierced my eyes. I turned my head and took a breath, thinking, 'John, John, three times the recovery rate. Your face is healing, light is going into the cheeks, the cells, the bones and blood system. Healing the scars and injuries to your face. The knives of the surgeon were accurate.'

"Stroke after stroke, I pictured John as I glided down the cold coastline of Mission Beach. After an hour and a half I had swum all the way from the lighthouse tower down to the end of the amusement park. By now the sun was down and I was cold. Testing my foot as I came into shore I knew I could run the mile or two I had swum down the coastline. With my soggy hair and thin, blue strapped leotard I felt full of life. I thought of my foot with the puffy swelling, 'Good God, Bill Emmerton ran across Death Valley minus a kneecap shot off in the war and his feet bandaged. This is nothing.' How can we stretch the limits of our consciousness unless we know the limits directly, through the body senses?

"I evoked the spirit of John running on the beach beside me. His clear eyes, his brilliant mind. The overlay of tragedy, of his aloneness and sorrow; yet, his childlike beauty. I ran two miles to the end of the beach and started back up again, toward the pier—another four miles. Though I ran almost without any effort, when I got within twenty yards of the pier fatigue hit me. I began walking waist-deep through the water to remove the pressure from my foot until the cold drove me ashore. I ran up to the pier and touched it.

"On the way back I tried to run in the deep sand. Then in the wet sand. My foot was swelling, and the cold air was whipping around my body in the dark. Finally I got out of myself. It was as simple as that. I just said, 'Dear God, I have to get down that beach and I'm going to think about John again.' So I filled my body with as much love and concentration as I could and slowly started to jog, trying to come down on the outside of the heel around on the toe, to get the weight off the tender spot. After two or three minutes I got into a rhythm and pretty soon I was running past the houses, past the amusement park. Then a light appeared in the sky. It looked like two brilliant eyes and I thought it was an omen. For a split second as I watched, it seemed like a mystical extraterrestrial object, but it was a plane.

"Far down the beach I saw the silhouette of the lifeguard tower, like a launching pad from another civilization. After an hour-and-a-half swim, a six-to-eight-mile run with an intestinal disorder and a lymph infection, I knew I hadn't hurt myself. My feet were warm now and I found my pink robe, my towel. John's consciousness was deeply in my body. I was blending with the most loving essential life force, concentrating all my healing energy on him. The next morning, as I woke in the comfort of my house, I realized not only had I healed John (whose recovery rate *was* three times the usual), I had also healed myself."

Healing Methods in a Running Culture

The Tarahumara Indians of northern Mexico are a primitive tribe with a deep knowledge of running trances and their healing properties. They hold hundred-mile races on high holy days and are expert trail runners.

Playwright Antonin Artaud, who spent several weeks with the Tarahumara in the 1930s and participated in the Tarahumara healing rites, observed these underlying assumptions in the Indian cosmology: (1) an active identification of the world as a geometric unity to which the human body is intrinsically related; (2) an equal embracing of the *masculine* and *feminine* aspects in nature; (3) a deep understanding of the role of the unconscious as "a powerful force that can repair their bodies when fatigued, give them strength, resistance to, and contempt for physical pain, injury and weakness."

Tarahumara healing rituals are rituals of movement.

Usually participants must endure an entire night of dancing without rest—and often these ceremonies are preceded by long runs through the surrounding forests. While in a trancelike state, the initiate envisions himself at one with the universe, being devoured by it, as though all the forces of nature were sucking out his illness and fatigue. In Tarahumara healing:

> The hierarchical order of things dictates that, after passing through the *ALL and the many,* one returns to the simplicity of the one, only to dissolve and be reborn by means of this process of mysterious assimilation. This dark reassimilation is contained within Ciguri, as a myth of reawakening, then of destruction, and finally of resolution in the sieve of supreme surrender, as their priests are incessantly shouting and affirming, in their Dance of All the Night. It lasts the whole night, from sunset to dawn, but it gathers the entire night as one gathers all the juice of a fruit at the very source of life.

The Tarahumara first exhaust their "conscious" reality in all-night dancing and distance running. Then, when the unconscious is open and receptive, they envision a mystical merging with the universe, and a total surrender to a greater healing power.

More recently, Dr. Irving Oyle, founder of the Headlands Healing Service in Bolinas, California, went to study the healing rituals of the famed "running culture." "The medicine men transmit religious or magical powers through ritual," he reports, "[and in this case] the dominant hemisphere receives the information, processes it and accepts or rejects the ritual as truth." The physical symptom may actually be a message from the body to the linear, rational, dominant hemisphere of the brain to stop all ego-centered activity, Oyle concludes.

The word "healing" means to make whole, to accept

one's total being without judgment, self-criticism, negative thoughts, or fears. With the mental imagery of the run we are creating a *new* ritual—as we leave our habitual shell of being with all our ego-centered worries and participate in a larger reality that contains the possibility for self-healing and the psychic power of our "perfect" body forms.

ELEVEN

Runner's Cosmology: From the Physical to the Metaphysical in a Moving Universe

---

A Return to the World View of the Greeks

With the running revolution in full swing we are rediscovering the full value of physical movement as it contributes to our psychological well-being, broadens our understanding of the world we live in, and illuminates our place within the cosmic scheme. At the same time we are beginning to revalidate those assumptions about the unity of body, mind, and soul and man's interaction with the dynamic forces of the universe that formed the underpinnings of Greek cosmology more than 2,000 years ago.

According to Plato, man occupied the central place in a hierarchy of motion, ranging from the limited and random shifts in the lower rungs of nature to the lawful, ordered orbits of the planets. The way he moved physically was considered key to his inner harmony. And by imitating the movements of the spheres, man could foster those emotions within that were naturally akin to the divine:

> The best motion is that produced in the self, by the self, which has most affinity with the movement and thought of the universe as a whole. Motion produced by another is worse, but worst of all is that in which the body lies

passive and its several parts are set in motion by other agents.

TIMAEUS (88–89)

On a practical level, Plato is saying that man can reach his highest potential only by willfully imposing order and discipline in his everyday actions. If he goes through life passively, continually reacting to outside stimuli, he will lack a spiritual and emotional center. Further, those who rarely move at all will have little sense of life, for the universe is known and understood only by our participation in its dynamic laws.

The sacred dances of the Greeks were designed to translate order into action. Every step was symbolic of internal harmony and each gesture made with regard to a spiritual and psychological center—the self. Smooth, rhythmical motions were signs that the individual lived in consonance with his philosophy. It is reported that Socrates, when asked how he kept his mental faculties so acute, replied, "I dance every morning," while one scholar claims that these ritual movements were really the dance of running and a Hellenistic variation on jogging in place!

In the sixth century B.C. the relationship of the body to the disposition of the soul was not a matter for debate but for direct experience. Moreover, the individual and the entire cosmos were thought to be governed by the same principles of central order and harmonic relation. Hence man's physical actions were also considered the measure of his understanding of the universe.

Now 2,000 years later, we're rediscovering the importance of our own physical movement as the basis for our interpretation of the world around us. And we're creating a new and more sophisticated cosmology to describe our interaction with the matter and mind-stuff of the universe.

Modern Cosmology and the
Mystical Mind-Space of the Run

While the Greeks believed that man could draw forth the wisdom of the heavens by imitating their lawful and ordered movements, today we believe we can make contact with a meaningful primary reality that transcends time and space in the meditative aspects of the run.

Though this may sound more like science fiction than scientific fact, physicist David Bohm of the University of London has proposed that the universe is actually a hologram: a matrix of circulating electromagnetic waves caused by the constant vibration of matter. Even our own flesh and bones disappear when highly magnified and what is left is an electromagnetic field that changes with the course of time. Further, our physical being is continually affected by the electrical impulses circulating in the universe as a whole. Hence, we are not just a collection of organs and parts but a cosmological system interacting with the universe at large.

Itzhak Bentov, a Boston biomedical consultant who uses the holographic model of the universe to explain altered states of consciousness, suggests that thoughts and ideas are vibrating, too, just the same as matter, but at a higher rate. According to Bentov, we can become aware of this high-frequency reality, akin to Plato's world of forms and essences, and read out the thought waves of the universe when we put ourselves into a deep meditative state.

When we run long distances we may *automatically* become attuned to these upper registers of reality. While we activate the archetypes of primal running man and the information code for our genetic and evolutionary past as we run, at the same time we reach a transcendental state that may enable us to connect with other forms of consciousness flowing through the universe at large.

As we open up to altered states of consciousness in the run, our body cells and brain waves are interacting with other electromagnetic fields circulating in the universe. Accordingly, we are moving toward a new psychology of being that takes into account this interface of the self as a pulsating wave with other thought waves in the universe, which we may identify as "archetypes" or as energy sources that influence the psychic development of the individual from "without."

Freud originally conceived of the psyche as a self-contained system with a constant amount of energy continuously exchanged between the various components—the ego, the id, and the superego. But Jung foresaw the marriage of physics and psychology and proposed an expansion of the basic model which was influenced by "archetypes" or energy sources from without.

The first thing that happens in the meditative aspects of the run—after we've been running for almost an hour—is that we begin to activate the more ancient parts of the brain and bring them into phase with the more recent layers of the psyche. Man has literally been "out of synch" as long as he's been sedentary, alienated from his own natural rhythms and also from the pulses of the universe. But as we run, we restore our inner harmony—the prerequisite for connecting with higher forms of consciousness and beginning to resonate with the universal mind.

The diagram on the following page shows the different levels of man's consciousness which come into harmony during the meditative moments of a long-distance run. Level one includes the genetic information for the evolution of all planetary life, including the evolution of man as a species; level two represents our inherited familial and genetic traits; level three is our personal history, the composite of

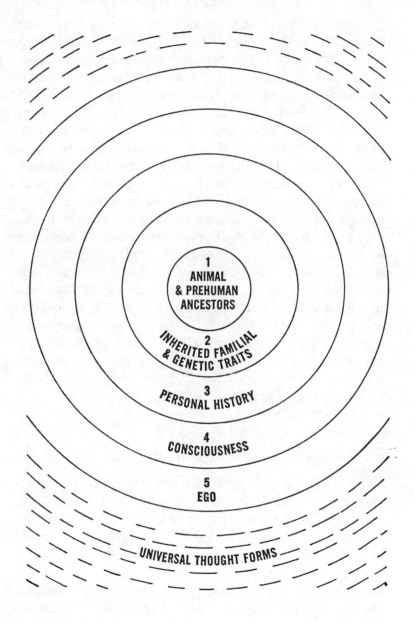

1
ANIMAL
& PREHUMAN
ANCESTORS

2
INHERITED FAMILIAL
& GENETIC TRAITS

3
PERSONAL HISTORY

4
CONSCIOUSNESS

5
EGO

UNIVERSAL THOUGHT FORMS

thoughts, feelings, and emotions that characterize our present life; level four is our awareness of the world around us; and level five is our consciousness of the self or ego.

"Outside" of the human psyche we have those thought frequencies described by Bentov as the fundamental data bank of thought forms flowing through the universe at large. From this model you'll notice that what we think of as our own identity—"ego"—actually exists on a very thin band between our inherited reality (levels one through four) and the outer world of universal thought forms. In the meditative moments of the run, we experience not only a heightened state of consciousness but a change in the very nature of our being. For as we synchronize our inner core with this outer reality of thought forms, we no longer see ourselves as the "possessors" of our bodies and our minds. Instead the ego appears to us as a thing "outside" the self, and we are able to watch the flow of our emotions and self-indulgent fears with the same dispassionate objectivity we once reserved for the examination of our biological processes and our abstract thoughts. In short, we reach a state where the ego no longer interferes with our ability to function as compassionate human beings behaving in a truly "selfless" manner.

Movement and the Collective Mind

When we reach this state with other runners, we experience a new kind of intimacy, for a kind of synchronous bonding takes place at the deepest level of our psyches. As you've undoubtedly experienced, it's possible to go farther and faster than you ever have before when you link up with a group of other runners, for there is a fund of collective energy—both physical and psychological—that sustains the group as a whole and from which the weakest runner can draw new strength.

Jeff Kamen, a reporter for WPIX-TV News in New York, began to explore altered states of being with India's guru Sri Chinmoy and soon was running three-mile workouts and meditating as he ran. When, despite his low mileage and a bout of severe knee pain, Kamen ambitiously entered a thirteen-mile race held to celebrate the guru's birthday, he found himself stumbling at the five-mile mark. Sri Chinmoy and the rest of the running group saw Kamen struggling and began to meditate on his finishing, visualizing a special energy push to get him around every curve in the roadway. Kamen imagined opening up and merging with the other runners. "With the help of my spiritual brothers," he recalls, "I was able to run the entire thirteen miles."

What is this powerful connection with other people in the meditative aspect of the run? According to biologist Lewis Thomas, it is the collective will of the species. Thomas tells us that all members of the animal kingdom, including man, are guided by a collective purpose which enables them to function not only as individuals but as component parts of nature. "Although we are by all odds the most social animals," Thomas writes, "we do not often *feel* our conjoined intelligence." This may be because we have stopped moving together and hence have lost our psychic identity as a group.

Thomas further speculates that the collective purpose for mankind is related to our ability to communicate and exchange information on higher wavelengths. "Perhaps we are linked in circuits for the storage, processing, and retrieval of information," he explains, "since this appears to be the most basic and universal of all human enterprises."

We do know that as people move together, they become "entrained"—exhibiting similar rates of psychic growth and biological change. It now seems possible that this entrainment may provide the basis for an evolving network of extrasensory communication and spontaneous thought exchange. Scientists in the Soviet Union researching telepathy and ESP believe that we may be developing a "single linked-species nervous system" which facilitates nonverbal communication and an instantaneous transfer of thoughts. We really do establish a "resonance" connection" with other people as we run, a kind of synchronization of consciousness based on our shared movements. Hence, as more and more people take up distance running, we may be evolving biologically toward some higher state of consciousness where we link up with universal thought forms and where extrasensory communication can occur!

Have we begun to lift the veil from ancient references to the relationship of our own harmonic movements with the motion of the spheres? In the meditative aspects of the run we are swept out of the mechanistic Newtonian universe and once again enfolded in the organic cosmos of the Greeks, where all matter is alive and vibrating in a rhythmic cosmic dance. As we run, our actions provide us with the things we need to understand the world around us: a system of gathering and ordering sensory information as well as an extrasensory way of intuiting our basic unity with the cosmos and our interaction with the physical forces within it. Thus we may experience the mysteries of the universe in the rhythmical motions of the run if we follow Plato's visionary advice:

> The motions that are naturally akin to the divine within us are the thoughts and revolutions of the universe. These each man should follow.

TWELVE

Creativity and Success: How Running Builds Self-Confidence and Brain Power

Man is, by design, a distance runner. Because our ancestors could outrun any other land animal over long stretches they were able to outstrip their closest competitors in the Pliocene forest. Now, three million years later, our heritage as distance runners remains key to our survival in the marketplace, for a regular program of jogging activates the physical and psychological characteristics required for success.

Because runners stress the heart and lungs at a constant rate, slowly building the body's capacity for oxygen utilization, they achieve greater physical endurance and more prolonged mental acuity. Not only do they have the stamina to work hard and put in longer hours, they are also more imaginative than their sedentary counterparts and are rapidly becoming a professional elite. According to a recent demographic study of the nation's top marathoners, over 50 percent earn more than $15,000 a year, and 96 percent have college degrees, and hold high-level positions in business, education, the sciences, and law.

You don't have to run a marathon, however, to develop the staying power and determination required for success. When the Tyler Corporation in Dallas initiated an eight-mile relay race to promote fitness among business leaders, they discovered that as executives trained, they developed the stick-to-it-iveness that company track records are made of. Tyler vice-president Fred Meyer believes that running builds perseverance and problem-solving abilities and also instills the long-term goal orientation necessary for planning a successful career. Chief operating officers of Mc-Graw Hill, Memorex, and Citibank—participants in the Tyler Cup race—now indicate they're more likely to hire runners over other candidates who are as professionally qualified but not as physically fit.

Results were improved morale, better attendance, and more work done per man-hour when Bonne Bell—makers of skin-care products for women—installed a track and exercise room in its Ohio headquarters. Its president, Jess Bell, turned out seasoned joggers in three months by offering employees a generous incentive of $1 for every mile they ran on company time. Moreover, Bell's way of doing business is indicative of the trend away from the two-martini executive lunch. The sales staff shows up in warm-up suits and clients bring their running shoes and stay for a dietetic lunch in the company cafeteria.

The new generation of job seekers is now picking up on running as an effective indicator of self-starting abilities. One young woman listed her college running on her résumé along with her academic credentials and got snapped up by a New York publisher impressed by the fact that she had organized the first women's track team at her prestigious college. When a group of Dartmouth and Williams graduates staged "Jogging for Jobs"—a thirty-six-hour marathon of résumé-dropping to New York advertising agencies—they received network news coverage and lucrative job offers for displaying those qualities that Madison Avenue holds most dear: imagination and hustle.

How does running foster the mind-set for achievement and build a model for success? As we run, we establish an "engram" in the circuits of the brain—a "picture of success" that serves as the motivating force behind all our creative efforts. The old saw, "Nothing succeeds like success," is really biologically based, for as we run and achieve the first goal man was meant to achieve, we activate the neuronal pattern for success that influences our performance of other more complicated tasks.

Our ability to activate this success "memory" is what makes the difference between proceeding with an air of self-confidence, thereby doing something well, and tackling a project with unnecessary trepidation, invoking automatic self-defeat.

"You feel so good for just having done it," explains Atlanta architect John Portman, who designed runners' paths around his Peachtree Center complex. "Running gives you the self-confidence to attack any problem—creative or financial—and sets you up for the rest of the day." Actress-author Shirley MacLaine jogs five miles on a treadmill every morning, whether she's onstage at Caesar's Palace in Las Vegas, filming in Hollywood, or secluded in her New York apartment at work on a forthcoming book. "It's a way of life," says Shirley, whose running is a ritual that invokes the discipline required for her multifaceted career.

According to Metropolitan opera star Robert Merrill, just two miles every morning is enough to put the picture of success into the forefront of your thinking—and to translate positive thinking into positive *action*. "Success is always easier for those who are accustomed to conquering," the baritone insists. Merrill attacks the hills near his Westchester home, assaults airport runways, or jogs around his hotel suite when on tour.

Building a Model for Success

How can you make your running serve as a model for success that spills over into the rest of your life? First, make a *commitment* to run for a certain period of time every day, regardless of how fast you run or how proficient you look. The only way to become successful at anything is to plunge in without worrying about your standards of perfection. Emerson once wrote, "You will have the power if you simply do the thing." First you build endurance; speed and a more refined technique will follow. Set aside a half hour every morning and keep jogging for as much of that time as possible. If you have to drop back to a walk at the beginning, fine. But keep moving for as much of the thirty minutes as you can.

Start slow and never push. If you've never jogged before, don't expect to go out and run for an hour at a time, at a seven-minute pace per mile, even if you *are* an ex-Marine. And don't start off at your fastest pace—you'll not only have to stop and walk sooner, but you may have to humbly hail a taxi to your door. Don't be afraid to adjust your goals downward in the beginning if you take on too much too soon. Remember, the way to use your running as a model for success is to first allow yourself to be successful at it. So forget about Kenneth Cooper's dictum that to be in perfect health you have to run two miles in fourteen minutes.

Run well within yourself. Your target should be between 50 and 75 percent of your maximum effort. You can tell you're properly paced if you can talk or hum to yourself as you jog.

Let this be the time your body decides when to speed up or slow down.

Part of a regular program of running is learning to trust your own internal process to get you where you need to go.

Instead of running your laps or your life according to an authoritarian system of rules and regulations, you learn to be sensitive to your own pacing—and these insights into your physical and psychological rhythms will serve you in your creative efforts as well.

Designer Oleg Cassini, who uses running to tune into his own individuality, says it's important to have time during the day to simply listen to yourself. "If you think about other people and their opinions first," he explains, "you will always be mediocre. I always run alone and stay just one step ahead of the competition."

After you've run for three weeks without any thought of speed or distance—and without the cumbersome self-criticism that causes so many to become "fitness drop-outs" —you can begin to use your running as a goal in itself, as a safe enclosed environment to push beyond your present capabilities and to use your daily workouts for personal growth and self-expansion. Start a runner's log and set up a two-pronged system of accounting. First, write in your maintenance goals—the number of miles you have to run per week in order to keep your present level of fitness. Next, write in your incentive goal: the number of miles you would like to work up to in the next six-week period. (To be practical, this goal should not exceed 40 percent of your present mileage.) Should you become fatigued or overstressed, simply drop back to your maintenance mileage for two weeks, then push ahead with your incentive goals once more, after you've rested. It should soon be apparent to you that however close you've come to achieving your incentive, it becomes easier and easier to raise your maintenance level. Every athlete knows that the way to develop a muscle is to coordinate stress workouts with short recovery periods.

The will is also a muscle that needs to be regularly stretched. When marathoner Paul Fetscher applied the maintenance/incentive method to his real estate career, scheduling a high-pressure round of sales calls to bring in new business every other month. Fetscher increased his commissions and discovered the psychic energy to begin a vitamin business on the side.

Finally, think of your training program as an "experiment of one." Take a moment to jot down in your journal or runner's log how you felt before and after your workout. And whenever you're tempted to skip a day, read over the previous entries. When you see how much better you've felt physically—and what a sense of accomplishment you've achieved—that should be motivation enough for you to lace on your shoes and forget about ill-founded excuses.

The beauty of distance running as a goal in itself is that it sets up a dialogue between you and possibility, between what you are and what you can be. It provides a model for developing self-confidence and the ability to risk—to push beyond what you think you can do and move closer to your true potential.

Just after finishing the Boston Marathon, thirty-nine-year-old Mary Gordon left a sinecure as vice-president of the Chase Manhattan Bank to recapture the trial and challenge of the race by pioneering a new field for women: investment counseling. As Mary planned for the marathon, she began to reevaluate her long-term career goals as well. She discovered a reservoir of strength in her limbs as she crossed the finish line after twenty-six miles. "If I can do that," she thought, "then I can do *anything.*"

Whenever we make a change in the body, we incur changes of equal magnitude in the mind. Once you learn you're capable of giving more of your body than you thought, you'll discover untapped sources of creative energy as well.

Sound unbelievably simple? Most of us need to be reminded of the relationship between hard physical effort and achievement—especially when our perspective is clouded by office politics and promotions that result from who you know, not what you do. Yet running reinforces the conviction that you can succeed—if you're willing to go the distance—and it builds a kind of personal integrity as well. *New Times* publisher George Hirsch, a marathoner since age thirty-four, credits runners with a certain ability for naked self-appraisal. It's clean and honest. "In distance running there's nothing left to luck or chance. There's no 'psyching out' of your opponent. There are no low blows or shortcuts, as there are in football and team sports. And it's not like tennis where the ball can be barely 'on the line.' "

In any career, you can take all sorts of shortcuts, but you can't deceive yourself with running. Too many people wake up and find they've been coasting along on a few lucky breaks. Others are too intimidated by the competition to even try. But running sets up a dialogue between you and possibility, and teaches you to view your own success as a straight and narrow road, uncluttered by other people's expectations or the vicissitudes of circumstance.

Building a Success Image

So many of us have dreams of changing jobs or becoming more successful at what we do but allow ourselves to be stifled by thoughts of our own inadequacies. Now you can change this by meditating on the "new you" and on your own success in problematic situations during the daily run. This is because as you exercise you are flushing out body tensions and silencing the analytical, self-critical segment of the brain—the "Who me?" inner voice that inhibits you and holds you back from trying.

In order to succeed at anything, we have to link right

action with right thought, and a relaxed and fluid body with an open, receptive mind. Whenever we think the very words "I can't," we cause contrary muscles to contract and thus work against the very thing we hope to accomplish. Similarly, if we hold a negative image of our own abilities, we will cause our self-confidence to contract and so speak and act in a less effective manner. But running teaches direct and forthright action and elicits an unencumbered mind.

The techniques for imagining yourself as a success go all the way back to the primal run, when early man identified himself with the hunting god as he went into the forest in pursuit of game. The hunter would visualize a successful kill and take on the persona of the deity as he stalked his prey. We, too, can invoke greater powers if we visualize our success and hold it in a fixed constellation of thought that illumines every action.

Running heightens our powers of creative visualization and gets the imagination working on the details of success. Most routine tasks require us to think critically and analytically and rely on the left or dominant hemisphere of the brain. But creative visualization draws on the right or intuitive hemisphere. The best way to suspend the screening function of the left brain is to give it some easy, repetitive task to monitor. Hence, running conveniently occupies the left brain, leaving the right brain free to indulge in guided fantasy.

So, if you're going into a new and unfamiliar job situation, use your running time to fantasize a virtuoso performance down to the last details. In your mind, create the "picture" of success. Don't analyze what it is you have to say and don't go over past mistakes. Whatever your goals, to succeed at speech-making, to feel confident as you ask for a raise, or make a presentation to a client, run along *as if*

you had already fulfilled them and imagine yourself successful and secure in your new role. When you actually get
into the situation, you'll say the right things instinctively
and assume a fluid, natural pose because you've already assimilated the mind-set and built in the body feelings that
accompany success.

Another way to work the idea of success into your body
movements and recount your past achievements is to run
in a slow, relaxed manner. Jim Clay is a forty-five-year-old
psychologist who tallies up every accolade of his academic
career as he jogs. He adds up the A's he got in graduate
school, then totals the dollar value of the scholarships he's
received. Sara Kravitz, a divorce lawyer, regularly recon-
structs her winning presentations in court—which guarantees her at least an hour's worth of running after a heavy
hearing schedule.

You can also bring the vision of success into harmony
with the body by using a jogging mantra. Think of a short,
positive statement about yourself or your ideal and then
breathe it into the movement of your body as you run.
Mantras should be roughly seven syllables, short, and to
the point. (If you have one from a meditation class, use
that.) The idea of building success into the rhythms of the
body is so universal that most of us learned how to do this
as children. The classic motivator for kids is still, "I think
I can, I know I can," puffed out by the "Little Engine That
Could."

You can also use the tunes of martial music as a nonverbal mantra or mentally run through the pulsing rhythm
of your college "fight" songs. Marvin Kale, a San Diego
businessman, jogs every morning with a headset and built-in
transistor radio and has even called the local radio station to
request the rousing overture to *Aida* and Wagner's *Twilight
of the Gods!*

Increasing Your Brain Power

The regular, repetitive movements of the run also lead us into a twilight mental state—similar to the moments just before sleep when we can unlock the powers of suggestive learning and overcome psychological resistance to difficult subject matter.

An enterprising company markets tape cassettes designed to teach us everything from foreign languages to the principles of accounting in these barely waking moments while we lie propped up in a cozy chair or languish in bed. Yet most of the purchasers fell asleep before they can absorb the contents because they were unable to keep their bodies in this equilibrium between full-blown analytical consciousness and sleep. We can enter and sustain the same free-floating frame of mind, however, where the mind can process large chunks of information more efficiently, by simply jogging for a half hour at a time at a slow, relaxed pace.

Singer Robert Merrill uses his jogging time to memorize music and go over operatic scores in his head. To organize her thoughts, traveling consumer advocate Bess Myerson jogs before she has to give a speech. Jim Jensen, anchorman for the CBS-TV news in New York, uses his running time to work on problems that his conscious mind is blocking. Jensen got A's in college physics but confesses to a mental block in math. "Now while I'm running, I do a little mental exercise," he explains. "I count up the men jogging at the gym, figure out their total weight, then their total speed, and what would be their total momentum if they hit the wall."

Sir John Eccles, the Nobel Laureate in physiology, wrote that the way to the imagination—the highest level of mental experience—lies through the lower levels of sensory experiences, imagery and memory. As we run, the brain is stimulated by the impressionistic blending of light and color, by a spectrum of Nature's sounds and harmonies, by the continuous streaming of body feelings, including the subtle movement of the air against the surface of the skin. These body feelings trigger associations from the past, and soon memories and related images flash across the field of inner vision. The sum total of these sensations is the crystal of creative thought. During these moments, we are not consciously trying to problem-solve. In fact, we are usually not even thinking of anything in particular but simply, as Emerson said, "allowing the thought to think itself." Our bodies and our minds become the canvas for the creative process, and our receptivity is heightened and expanded in the run.

Bertrand Russell once said that the greater part of creativity is often the nonthinking time, when the subconscious is free to randomly sift through the data banks of the brain and pick up pertinent facts. "If I have to write on some rather difficult topic," Russell explained, "the best plan is to think about it with very great intensity—the greatest intensity of which I am capable—for a few hours or days and, at that time, give orders, so to speak, that the work will proceed underground. After some months I return consciously to the topic and find that the work has been done."

Novelist Joseph Heller explains that his best ideas come when he is away from the typewriter, and he puts in 360 laps at a nearby YMCA on his lunch hour. "Running puts me in a free-floating frame of mind where random bits of dialogue coalesce into major scenes," Heller acknowledges. He also finds the isolation of running is a boon for creative thinking—"I make it very clear to people that I am not there to socialize"—and notes that the repetitive nature of the laps adds even more to the imperturbable reveries of his meditation.

If you want to problem-solve as you run, it's important not to run too fast, but to keep to a speed that's only 50 to 60 percent of your maximum capacity. If there's too much physical strain, the brain will be too occupied with regulating your physiological responses and you won't get into a free-floating state of mind.

Run slowly, too. It takes about twenty minutes to get rid of your body tensions and enter the "problem-solving state." To be really successful with this method, stay on your feet for at least half an hour.

It's best to run alone in order to get into the inner-directed state where the creative process can take over. Let your body become "a room of one's own"—a place where you can withdraw from ringing telephones and the pressures and demands of other people.

Don't talk to anyone on your way out the door. Use the five or ten minutes before you run to center on your problem. Read over all the relevant material for the task at hand. Then sit still with your eyes half closed, breathing deeply and slowly. Start your run with a "soft focus" on the outer world and think of bringing your energies inward.

Next, follow Russell's Rule: don't attempt to consciously solve the problem. Let your imagination have free rein and simply observe your thoughts and watch the interplay of images and memories as they move across your mental canvas.

While some executives and writers are able to dictate or sit down at the typewriter as soon as they finish their run, others find it handy to carry a small tape recorder or Dictaphone with them. If you do, strap it around your chest or waist and make certain the weight is balanced.

If the answer to your question doesn't pop out during or

after the run, you might need another dose of twilight imagery in order to unravel your dilemma. In that case, pose the problem to yourself once again before you go to bed. Get up slowly the following morning and ease into your run. Frequently answers that don't come to us during working hours come to daylight in our dreams. And runners do dream more vividly and more often because intense aerobic exercise induces deeper states of sleep.

Try not to talk to anyone in the morning or to make even the smallest decision until you've had your run. You want to stay as close as possible to the semiwaking state you're in when you roll out of bed, and use your workout to recall the wisdom of your dreams. Then come back and sit quietly for a few minutes with pen in hand—and let your ideas flow.

Cardiologist George Sheehan, who writes a column on running for his hometown paper every Wednesday, uses this technique. "On Monday I run ten miles and think about my column and if the ideas don't come, I sleep on it," he explains. "Then I run the first thing Tuesday morning. By then the article has usually written itself."

A way of marshaling additional support during your creative run is to envision yourself jogging with a committee of mental mentors—people whom you admire and who share some sympathy for your work. A woman novelist runs alternatively with George Sand and Virginia Woolf and holds imaginary conversations on the elements of style. And at UCLA Berkeley, there's a physicist who calls theoretical conferences with his colleagues in the East when he's plagued with a knotty problem.

This technique of dialoguing is only another way of loosening up and preparing yourself to receive the wisdom that's hidden within the recesses of your mind. It's an indirect way of jogging the imagination and evoking problem-solving powers without encouraging a conscious manipulation of the facts.

Running As an Antidote to Overthink

William James once wrote that modern man was too tense and worried to be successful with his creative efforts.

When you find yourself getting flustered, it may be because your brain is jammed with too many disconnected insights and ideas and you need to slow down your thoughts to put them into proper sequence. John Harnad, a professor at UCLA, jogs in place when his thoughts begin to come too fast and furiously to make any sense. "After twenty minutes, my body and mind have come together and I find I'm thinking at a much more digestible rate."

Your mental and physical pacing begin to work together as you jog; the body slows the mind and establishes a much more manageable narrative of thought.

Running, more than any other exercise—mental or physical, releases nervous tension and clears away interfering thoughts, enabling you to center on the issues at hand.

I first learned about the problem-solving benefits of running when given a rush assignment to write a magazine article about Château Prieure-Lichine, a sixteenth-century priory and vineyard I had visited on a wine tour of France. With the deadline thirteen hours away, I had no leads, just a lot of unusable anecdotes and notes. In desperation I went down to the track and numbly ran twenty laps. As I began to breathe deeply and relax, I found the introduction taking form, and by the time I'd finished running, I'd outlined the entire article in my head. As I finished my workout, I avoided speaking to any of my friends, wishing to guard this state of mind and keep it intact until I reached my desk. I sat down and miraculously typed out, word for word, the narrative that came to me as I ran.

Running As an Antidote to Overwork

It's important to stick to your running schedule in order to combat the buildup of negative emotions and body tension that can stem the flow of creative thought and halt your productivity at work.

We need to run more than ever when we are under pressure, though it seems that's when we can least afford to take the time. The body absorbs tension during the working day, and if you don't take the time to flush it out, you'll buckle more easily under stress. Larry Kramer, president of a Chicago advertising agency, explains how running keeps him from getting mentally and physically unglued. "When one of our big proposals was rejected I decided to call top management and tell the client they were making a big mistake. As I was practicing my speech I lost my nerve and felt shooting pains down my arm. By the time I went to bed I had all the classic signs of nervous stress." Larry got up at one o'clock in the morning and ran ten miles. "I just kept on going," he explained, "until I got the devils out. While I didn't get the account, I did get rid of the shakes and avoid getting sick with tension."

Tension in the body—if unattended to—can easily disrupt the creative process and leave you even further behind. Even if you're under the most impossible deadlines, you have to consider running time a way to keep your body relaxed and your mind in working order.

Ken Gilmore is a magazine editor who routinely put in fifteen-hour days until he became crippled by severe tension headaches. After spending $10,000 on doctors, physiotherapy, and massage, all to no avail, Gilmore stumbled on running as a sure-fire relief.

If you're suffering from an acute bout of work-induced tension, take a slow run at least thirty minutes in length. Check your body for tension points. Unclench your teeth. Jog with a limp jaw and let your bottom lip hang. Drop your shoulders and unclench your fists; let your arms fall loosely at your sides. Concentrate on breathing the tension out of your body as you run. If you're angry with someone at work, imagine that you're kicking your anger out through your heels. Mary K, an executive secretary, admits to sometimes imagining that she's stomping on her boss's face.

Groaning out loud also releases tension. You can exert 10 to 15 percent more physical strength as you run if you bellow now and then. And you can double your mental strength by jogging and clearing out the harpies that are gnawing at your nerves.

Like the marathon, a career is a journey of self-actualization from where we are to where we wish to be. Running provides us with a powerful tool to alter self-image and build a model of success. It builds our physical reserves and fosters the psychological characteristics of self-discipline and determination necessary for sustained creative effort.

Yet most important, running also teaches us to look inward—to build our game plan for success on personal standards for self-gratification. So many of us look for external reasons to succeed—to accumulate possessions, power, or prestige—and are defeated by external causes— the long, hard hours required, increasing pressure to perform, and the routine nature of many job-related tasks.

The marathoner may spend months in arduous training, pushing harder and harder until he reaches his goal—to run twenty-six miles and get back where he started from —for no *objective* reason. Yet he gets tremendous satisfaction from his achievement, and the whole process holds tremendous *meaning* for him. He is completely inner-directed, and this self-direction makes him more independent, self-reliant, and self-sustained in every other aspect of his life. With an ever-present goal and a link to powers greater than himself, the runner never questions the significance of his own success but continues moving forward to achieve it.

THIRTEEN

Toward a New Androgyny: How Running Makes Women More Independent and Assertive

In the 1896 Olympics, àn adventurous young woman named Melpomene (after the Greek muse of tragedy) unofficially ran the marathon with a bicycle escort in a time of 4:30 and was never heard from again. Though the Greek sportswriters thought it unchivalrous to deny a woman's request to enter the race, it must be admitted that Melpomene was treading on sacred ground. As far back as 776 B.C. women were forbidden to set foot on the hallowed precinct of Olympia where the games were held, and the penalty for any female caught viewing these war maneuvers —where men ran the length of the stadium at the peril of spears and studded javelins—was instant death.

By the 1960s the Amateur Athletic Union of the United States had not advanced much beyond the ancient superstition that it was "bad luck" for women to compete. Separating the folklore from the facts, Nina Kuscsik, a registered nurse and the first woman to win the Boston Marathon, told the New York Academy of Sciences conference on the marathon in 1976 that women were recently denied access to any distance beyond the quarter mile because running would make them "muscle-bound" and such strenuous activity would be hazardous to their health. Accord-

158

ing to Kuscsik, for the fifty years following Melpomene's unheralded feat, women continued to graciously accept the word "no." Some—called "brazen doxies"—ran anyway, finding out their unofficial status as athletes by jumping into races after hiding in the underbrush, then noting the finishing time of the closest male runner. They didn't just jump into the easy races either: in 1959, twenty-nine-year-old Arlene Pieper completed a marathon by running up and down Pike's Peak. Still, these pioneers of women's distance running were discouraged by the sports establishment. One AAU official pointed to a starkly angular woman runner and admonished the rest of the field, "Look at her! Before she started running she used to be attractive."

When Women's Running Took Wings

Though we might expect the queen of the Amazons to have led the charge against the chauvinism of the Greeks, it was, in fact, a group of suburban housewives and mothers, mostly in their thirties and married to other runners, who fought for equal rights in the marathon. And their sergeant was Boston's Sara Mae Berman, a mother of two, who started jogging when she found out that the generally flabby condition most people have reached by the age of thirty is the condition they're likely to stay in for the rest of their lives. While Sara went from Sunday jogger to eight-mile workouts, then on to break the unofficial record of three hours for the women's marathon, Dr. Ernst van Aaken, a West German track coach, was predicting that over long distances of fifty to one hundred miles, women could outlast and even outrun the men.

Whenever it's a question of staying power over muscle power the supposedly weaker sex has an advantage since more of their body weight is stored fuel and less is dead

weight or muscle. When eighty-nine-pound Miki Gorman
finished the 1974 Boston Marathon with a 2:47 victory
(at an average speed of six and a half minutes per mile)
feeling fresh and chipper, she told a television interviewer,
"I can't run much faster, but I can run much, much farther."
Including a hundred miles around an indoor track, which
Miki did "for fun."

But in the days when the AAU thought running would
transform eighty-nine-pound ladies into Charles Atlases, or
at least into cronies who might kick sand in your face at
Muscle Beach, Christine MacKenzie, a British distance
runner with records for the thirteen- and twenty-six-mile
marks, went to the monthly AAU meeting clad only in a
coat and a bikini, and when the subject of muscles came
up, she dropped her coat to the floor and politely inquired if
the men thought her too "muscle-bound." Shortly thereafter she was given permission to run the quarter mile in
U.S. distance races. And women continued to sneak in their
longer runs as they once might have stolen an illicit ciga-
rette—though now they were denied what was better for
them under the pretext that it would be injurious to their
health and rob them of the strength they needed for repeated childbirth.

The issue of women's running was brought out in the
open in the 1967 Boston Marathon when Kathrine Switzer,
a Syracuse University coed, was issued a number and allowed to race because she had filled in the entry form with
her first initial only. The gun went off, a few miles into
the marathon Kathy removed her hooded sweatshirt, and
race organizer "Jock" Semple tried to physically drag her
off the course. A flying phalanx of Syracuse University
football players accompanied Kathy along with her then-
husband, a six-foot shotputter weighing 220 pounds. He
threw a classic block to Semple, allowing Kathy to finish

the race in just over three hours. Instead of a laurel wreath, Kathy faced expulsion from the AAU for four violations: she had run over one and a half miles; she ran with men; she fraudulently entered an AAU race; and she ran without a chaperone.

Kicked out of the AAU and into the arms of the media, Kathy created such a stir as a folk heroine that the AAU finally decided to relent and let women run the marathon as long as they had a course separate from the men's. In 1971, the Roadrunners Club, long boosters of women's running, adhered to these guidelines by starting the women's division of the New York City Marathon ten minutes earlier than the men's. When the gun was fired, the women calmly sat down and voluntarily added ten minutes to their time, then got up and began racing with the men. They also filed a lawsuit against the AAU for discrimination in a public place, and according to Nina Kuscsik, who ran five marathons that year, "Women's running took wings." That women were held back more by psychological and social restraints than by their inherent physical capabilities is evidenced in the rapid shave of thirty minutes off their world's record in the last ten years—as compared to a drop of barely twenty minutes in the men's record over the last forty years.

Running Through Psychological Barriers: Fears and Peer-Group Pressures

Today women under twenty-five have little idea what pressures their jogging sisters had to bear to secure their rights to the roadways. Female runners raised in the pre-lib era had to be even more willing to discount peer-group pressure and focus on their own individual goals. Then, the idea that a woman's body should be securely immobilized on its pedestal was still more widely held by women than by men. Our Victorian grandmothers thought that by avoiding exercise and staying pale they would cultivate the appearance of gentility, and it was feared that good facial color and a trim figure were a dead giveaway that one had to work for a living. Then, too, no woman was immune from the duties of motherhood, and the horror of the economic and physical woes of repeated childbirth caused many women to feign illness—fainting and fatigue, accompanied by a sickly pallor—in self-defense.

Once these social inhibitions began to fade, women over thirty simply internalized their parents' attitudes toward competition. Psychiatrist Carl Rogers explains that the father's encouragement, or lack of it, determined whether or not a girl would engage in sports, while the mother's approval was what instilled a willingness to compete. Some women marathoners, in their thirties, like Kathrine Switzer, had support from older brothers as well as from their parents. And they were strong enough to face the suspicions of their classmates that they were somehow too masculine as a result of their athletic pursuits. Then, too, they were able to reach the point where their general anxiety over competition was replaced by the satisfaction of performance. The countless women who have allowed themselves to be deprived of full body movement, and who've left that rambunctious run behind to the closed parenthesis of childhood, may find that once they start to run again all those internalized parental admonitions will begin to surface. One woman jogger in her thirties was startled by a dream in which her mother stood over her and said, "You'll never be a runner. You're just not any good."

Another, Brenda Donaldson, a physical education instructor in her early thirties, started jogging three times a week in conjunction with her psychotherapy. She discovered that running was a way of proving herself to men, trying to please her father, and make up for her younger brother's death. After working through these associations with her running, Brenda was able to do three miles for the sheer joy of it. "Now I'm running for myself," she says.

It also seemed that once women got the courage to combat their conditioning—to be physically weak and slow-footed—they frequently faced the most threatening experiences of their lives. When Kathrine Switzer first came to New York she frightened her friends and roommates by taking ten-mile workouts in Central Park or along the East River after dark. "I knew the park so well that I could tell the difference between the shadow of a bush, a man, or a tree," she maintains, "but late at night, especially if I were tired, I'd get paranoid and the bush would become a man with a cloak and dagger." Finally she worked out a mile-long course around her garden apartment on the East Side of Manhattan, and her boyfriend timed her, knowing if Kathy didn't make it back to the start in seven minutes, something would be amiss.

After several of these uneventful training sessions, Kathy took a run on an early April morning—one of her last fifteen-milers before the Boston Marathon. She heard someone behind her. A man in an old sweater and baggy jeans, appearing to be "just another jogger trying to pass that woman up ahead," pulled out a knife and stuck it to her throat. "I'm going to cut you," he said. Kathy perspired so profusely that the assailant's hand slipped from her neck. Then he kicked her in the stomach. She reached into her belt and pulled out an aerosol can of Mace and stood for one frozen moment as the vapor enveloped his face in slow motion—then dashed to a phone booth and called the police.

Most women report that they feel *less helpless* after

jogging because they know they can at least run away from a menacing situation. Then, too, statistics show that women runners are attacked in flight less often than they would be just walking through secluded areas. But to be safe, any runner should follow these basic rules: don't run where you wouldn't feel comfortable walking by yourself. Carry five dollars and identification on you at all times, plus a dime for a phone call. And run with someone if you're jogging late at night.

"Why Can't a Woman Be More Like a Man?"

Thanks to pioneers like Kathy Switzer and Nina Kuscsik, women today can freely indulge in sports like distance running without seeming to reject their femininity. As recently as the late 1960s, however, women athletes were thought to be trading in some aspect of the feminine selfhood, because personality tests administered to sportswomen were based on stereotyped ideas of sexual behavior. "Femininity" was gauged in terms of passivity and dependence, and "masculinity" in terms of aggressiveness and independence. Moreover, these tests were not calibrated to indicate any behavior in between these assumed norms. Thus a woman who engaged in physical competition—of any form—appeared as "masculine" and aggressive, and people worried that something was wrong with her glands or that something was "not quite normal about her."

Yet Dr. Dorothy Harris of Penn State University knew the deck had been stacked against the female athlete. So she found a method of diagnosing the degree of agency (the masculine instinct to be the "doer") and communion (the feminine instinct to yield or cooperate) in female runners. The results: in any situation, female joggers were likely to exhibit *both* impulses to the same degree. Thus they were apt to be androgynous without incurring any loss of femininity. And even more surprising, they showed higher self-esteem than women who tested out at the predominately "feminine" end of the scale.

Harris next began to focus on the components of athletic motivation among women runners, and learned that these same women who appeared to be "androgynous" had successfully assimilated those characteristics assigned to the male in our society: self-assertiveness, independence, and a solid work ethic—and what she called "personal unconcern." Women overly worried about their performance tend to withdraw from sports or any other competitive activities—and success belongs to the female who doesn't care what others think but sticks to her own strategy. Harris also found that women who said they'd rather not be involved in sports weren't achievement-oriented and had these valuable "masculine" qualities in short supply.

As women runners make major strides toward re-owning their own body power, they become psychologically more secure than their sedentary sisters. How does a program of regular training serve to implement the male intentionality or "logos" of a woman's mind? It seems the linear, purposive elements of her personality emerge in proportion to the time and effort she puts into her training. The perseverance and single-mindedness required to log upward of ten miles a week spill over into the rest of her life, enabling a woman to be more self-sufficient and direct. She quickly learns, as a result of her running, that progress is strictly a matter of effort and that the straight path is the shortest distance between two points, while most of her life she has been conditioned to think of herself as the beneficiary of someone else's goodwill and to take the least obtrusive and, frequently, the most circuitous route to achieving her desired ends.

In much the same way that men engage in competitive athletics to bolster their self-esteem, women are now running to gain self-confidence, a sense of their own physical strength and body power.

"I felt myself becoming stronger and stronger," says Stephanie Koenig, who finished last in the 1976 Maryland Marathon after jogging for only a month. "And afterward I recovered quite quickly, any stiffness was gone in two and a half days."

Even those women who were once terrified of being called "unfeminine" are beginning to jog to build their "body-ego" and muscle strength.

Laverne Paradise confirmed that as a child the idea of being a tomboy terrified her. "Now years later I'm reclaiming what is mine. I first laced my tennis shoes and jogged around the block a year ago. And I've since graduated to good running shoes and to yoga and regular workouts with weights. My muscles haven't started to bulge out all over. But I do feel I'm moving more upright and gracefully. My shoulders are stronger and, yes, I even go downstairs and flex in front of the mirror."

Women runners are also better able to cope with pain because they stress their bodies regularly. "When I had an IUD inserted for the second time, my physician warned me I might have severe cramps," reports a jogger in her thirties. "Though I experienced pain, it was considerably less than I expected. I expect my body to deal with stress and it does."

Most importantly, with a regular running program you can claim for your own those "androgynous" characteristics of self-mastery, perseverance, competitive spirits, and freedom from social approbation that once were considered the province of successful men.

First, start by finding out how far you can comfortably

run without tiring. Then set up a schedule of five training runs a week—make two of those 50 percent longer than your present distance. If you're only at a half-mile effort, you can safely stretch yourself to three quarters of a mile. If you're running two miles, push yourself up to three. Don't allow yourself to miss a day or cheat on your mileage. At the same time, don't push for speed and don't be self-critical. Just tell yourself you are running "for the experience." By the end of six weeks, you will have proven to yourself that you can straightforwardly work toward a goal and not make excuses or give up when your own performance doesn't meet your own idealistic standards.

William James observed that success or failure is judged in relative terms—and if the distance between your aspirations and your performance is too great, you're likely to get discouraged, which can dampen your spirits in the early competitive stage, and make you give up too soon.

So, choose your goals wisely. The rule of thumb for racing is that you can safely go 75 percent farther than you're used to running in your daily workouts. So, if you've been training at four miles at a stretch, you'll have no trouble finishing a seven-mile competition. You'll find there's an energy wave that carries through the crowd and adds a zesty kick to your own native abilities. Moreover, there are enough women's races—including the 6.2-mile mini-marathon—so that you should have no trouble finding a field of women and a race that's right for you. Once you've built up your self-confidence, you're ready to really sharpen your competitive spirit and develop the ability to risk.

While the woman who competes with men is still not wholly welcome in her liberated garb to games and contests that for years were the social pillars of a male society, no female timing herself on the first leg of a marathon is likely to suffer the humiliation that Susan Palmer did. When her college coach sent her in to replace a male center-forward in the last few minutes of the game, Susan's teammates showed their confidence in her ability to maintain the winning edge by stalking off the court.

Twenty-four-year-old Ellie McGrath at first was hesitant to enter what she thought of as the closed world of athletic competition. "As a child I was overweight and uncoordinated and terrible at racquet sports. Though I used to ride my bicycle and time myself, that was as competitive as I ever got. Then I started running to get in shape. The first time I showed up for a race I looked around at all the people in their warm-up suits and track club jerseys and thought, 'What am I doing here? I am *not* an athlete!' "

But encouraged by the special camaraderie characteristic of distance runners, as well as the lack of competitive pressure, she went on to complete her first marathon with less than six months' training. "People who were ostensibly competing with me in races would stop and say, 'I think you're holding your arms too high and you might be more comfortable if you dropped them.' Then they'd pick up their pace and go on by."

But the most impressive aspect of the marathon was the support the women gave each other. "I was running as part of a team and what kept me going was knowing that my friends, Laurie and Jane, were ahead of me. And we were all encouraged by the middle-aged housewives who came out on their husbands' arms to watch. Each time a woman runner passed they'd roar 'YOU CAN DO IT! YOU CAN WIN!' symbolizing all the years they'd sat in front of the TV while their husbands watched football and hockey and drank beer, and these were women who'd never even run a mile!"

As a result of competition, you'll instinctively develop

what Dorothy Harris called "personal unconcern"—the ability to set your own goals without being worried what other people will think.

After running the 6.2-mile mini-marathon in Central Park, I was met by a disparaging comment from a former boyfriend. "How come you ran so slow? Did you see all those people coming in ahead of you?" he said. I frankly admit my first impulse was to be "weak"—burst into tears. "How could he criticize me," I thought. "What did I do wrong?" Then suddenly something clicked. I realized (1) I had just finished running more than six miles on a day that I was exhausted, had a cold, and didn't want to get out of bed; and (2) it was an honest effort and I was proud of it. I had met my own objectives: to run in a field of 2,000 other women and enjoy finishing with my two best friends. And I just plain didn't care what anybody thought.

How This New Self-Assertiveness Spills Over into Your Social Life

Not surprisingly these airs of independence can carry over into your personal life, make you more self-sufficient and less demanding of your friends and lovers.

"I used to be a very dependent female," says Rosalie Prinze, a thirty-year-old divorcée who had gone from running ten to fifty miles a week over the last five years. "When I was married, I wanted my husband to spend more time with me. I had no consuming interests of my own and couldn't understand why he wanted to do things without me. But running changed all that."

What Rosalie developed through running was a sense of body-ego, physical self-assuredness. As she became more fit and more compact, she began to pull together psychologically and regain her personal power. "As I ran one morning, it came to me," Rosalie recalls. "An inner voice said, 'You're special,' and though there were other people crossing my path, they never entered my *space*. I could feel the edges of my body—it was as if my boundaries were consolidating—and I felt more *me*."

The metaphor of movement also proved an answer to the immobilization Rosalie felt on the analyst's couch as she attempted to work through those aspects of her own personality that contributed to the divorce. "My therapy helped, but my running helped me more. There are some things you learn intellectually, but running you learn in your *gut*." As Rosalie developed the self-discipline to increase her running to fifty miles a week, she also became more assertive in other aspects of her life and was able to end an unsatisfying affair. "When things were going well, my boyfriend wanted me there, and when they weren't he wanted me to go home. I got tired of this push/pull relationship and thought, "If running can be mine and mine alone, then there will be other things as rewarding.' I realized I didn't need to latch on to someone else to make me whole. Even being alone on Saturday night doesn't bother me the way it used to. One weekend my roommate was away and I hadn't made any plans. All I thought about was when I could run and when I could get to the health club for a sauna. The paranoia about being dateless is gone."

An athletic-looking blonde in her mid-thirties, Sue Finnerty is a reporter for *Time* magazine who found that running made her more self-assured during a difficult period of social readjustment. "I broke off with a man and decided to use the time I'd normally spend brooding to get back into shape," Sue explains. "He went to est and then walked out on me and it was just like someone died. Another man called me that week, but moving into another relationship didn't answer anything for me, and running did.

"I'm not sure it took me less time to get over the breakup," Sue admits, "but I did get rid of a lot of anger in my running. And I managed to get through this on my own without going into therapy or getting snagged by any of the fads. At the moment I'm in between relationships and I don't feel as lost as I would if I didn't have the physical outlet of running to rely on."

"I think most of us have gone through a period without dates or friends where we felt terribly isolated," says thirty-eight-year-old Janice Benton, a lithe redhead who started running to use up excess energy when she cut back to a three-day workweek. "What woman who lives alone hasn't walked into her apartment and said, 'Oh! I didn't make any plans tonight.' But where do you go—what do you do? Especially if you won't go to the singles bars because you've become vulnerable to the fact that you're alone and you're uptight about being approached by strangers?"

Janice, who holds jogging classes in New York four times a week, feels running is a step in the right direction. Though her classes cater to beginners of both sexes, more than half of her joggers are single women in their late twenties or early thirties who are looking for a way to get out of the house after work, as well as a way to stay in shape. They've found that pursuits such as creative writing classes or photography lessons are not as satisfying as running because they're not as active or as social. Jogging gets them out of doors and is the perfect antidote to the dateless indoor weekend blahs—as well as to the compulsiveness and self-indulgence intrinsic to a sedentary life-style.

In fact, most women runners find they've become less concerned with filling up the week with social engagements, especially when those evenings spent "biding time" can't compare with the physical highs of running.

"Unless I'm really in love with someone," says runner Terry Cox, "I don't want to give up any of the time or energy reserves I normally use in running."

Is it really better to run than to make love? Sometimes the answer is yes. "The feeling of timelessness and bodily suspension is almost guaranteed in a good long run," says Terry. "A man has to be pretty special to compete with that."

As they become more secure in their own physicality, women also begin to look at men in a different light. They're less concerned with gaining "attention" or "approval," and are able to defuse the sexual tension that too often colors every male-female social exchange. Kathy L, a twenty-nine-year-old jogger, confides, "I still find men attractive. I'm just not so worried whether they care or not. One night I was jogging in the park near dusk and I saw a man running at a nice pace, so I joined him. He was very handsome, and normally I'd have tried to get his number. By the time we'd finished running, I hadn't bothered to find out if he was married or had a girlfriend. I didn't even know his name!"

If you're a single woman and aren't dating because you're in between relationships, you're working hard, or don't have the time, or if you're in one of those periods where you want to meet someone desperately but can't, you can still treat yourself to feelings of body pleasure. Your running will make it easier to get through those periods when you're not being touched and caressed, or enjoying the streaming sensations of a regular sex life.

For years most of us have been taught to think of our bodies as giving pleasure to someone else. We've worried about our appearance for the sake of husbands and countless lovers, and tried to keep fit insofar as it would benefit our ability to take care of the home and work hard to support our families. It's not surprising, then, that the feelings of physical pleasure on a solitary run can also open a Pandora's box of guilt and self-recrimination, especially for those women who are used to basing their own happiness on the fulfillment of someone else's needs. "Whenever I'm having a good time and feeling free, I get a premonition of disaster," says one mother of three who trains for marathons and shorter distance races. "When I'm enjoying my running and thinking that my training is paying off, all of a sudden a disaster pops into my mind—like my child getting hit by a car. It's a very basic conflict. Consciously I know that what I'm doing is best for me—staying in shape and keeping fit—but unconsciously I feel I should be attending to someone else. Sometimes I even see things jumping out of the pavement—like knives. And I think how good I feel and how wretched these things are! I feel like I don't deserve all this pleasure. But the feeling passes and I say to myself, 'This is *my* playtime.' "

Pregnancy: How Running Conquers Fears of Helplessness and Dependency

While jogging allows you a momentary flight into your own private world—away from the demands and responsibilities of motherhood and family life—there are added benefits for women who keep jogging during pregnancy, such as a lessening of physical fears and dependency and faster recuperation with no postpartum blues.

Carol Dilfer was living on an American army base in Germany when she found herself pregnant with her second child. She started jogging because "I found myself lonely and missing movement. I was feeling stiff and grumpy from the lack of exercise and somehow the idea of sitting around for the last three months of my pregnancy and getting fat on German food was not at all appealing."

Carol joined a health club near the army post where she

met former Berlin track star Hilda Smith—then seven months' pregnant and jogging a mile and a half a day. "In her ninth month Hilda ran down the hill toward the dispensary and delivered her baby three hours later," says Carol. "Her stamina amazed me. In just two weeks she was back to the exercise classes at the club, pushing her baby buggy as she jogged her mile and a half."

After reading Kenneth Cooper's book, *Aerobics,* on men, Carol mistakenly went out and tried to jog a mile and a half in twelve minutes, "a pace too fast for a previously nonjogging, eight months' pregnant woman to maintain." When she slowed down to a twelve-minute mile, she found she could put in six miles a week, and after delivery there was no question that running had been a tremendous help. "I went into a long labor at 1:00 a.m. after a week-long bout with the flu. I expected to be totally exhausted, but instead I sat up and chatted with my friends an hour after delivery, took a shower, and never did experience that terrible fatigue immediately following childbirth."

Though she'd been told by friends and parents that pregnancy should be a quiet, contemplative period, Carol found that strong, firm, elastic bodies get through delivery more easily and that postpartum depression is quelled or eliminated with a continuous program of exercise carried over into the recovery period. "When I ran during pregnancy, I felt not only good but smug," Carol recalls, "especially with the army men jogging past me in their heavy boots. But *staying* in good physical shape is important in terms of realizing your on-going life purpose. Birth is over with in just twenty-four hours."

A convert to active pregnancy, Carol began holding fitness classes for pregnant women on the army base. When she and her family returned to Palo Alto, California, Carol set up the Prenatal and Postpartum Aerobic Fitness Program at the local recreation center. At eight o'clock in the morning, Carol's summer lawn class takes over the playing field in the affluent suburb of Menlo Park. Ten women spread out their calico quilts and are led through a series of gentle stretching exercises culminating in a slow folding of the body into the fetal position and five minutes of relaxed deep breathing and meditation. None has the fatty tissue or facial bloat so frequently associated with pregnancy. One young woman in jeans and an Indian print blouse reports, "I can really feel the power in my body. It's only at night when I take off all my clothes and stand in front of the mirror that I realize I'm pregnant." Far from being logy and lethargic, these women are exuberantly active. Diana, in her eighth month, is almost sleek in her baby-blue warm-up suit. "Once in a while, if I bend down to pick up the cat's dish after sitting for a time, I feel heavy and as though I'm carrying something separate. But after jogging a mile or more every day I feel like a gazelle."

Carol also includes exercises which strengthen the pelvic floor muscles that support the bladder, the uterus, and the lower intestine, as well as modified push-ups to build up the upper arms: "These are great for carrying backpacks full of groceries or small children," she encourages.

Her basic rules are:

Consult your obstetrician before you begin to jog. If you're having a normal pregnancy and your physician asks you not to run, you should have a satisfactory answer to why the doctor feels that way. You may find, too, that you have to shop around for an exercise-oriented doctor much the way you would for one who believes in natural childbirth or Lamaze delivery.

Plan a regular program of jogging and stick with it at least three times a week. Any less will not provide the desired aerobic training effect. Next, begin each session with a good warm-up of the major joint areas—the neck, shoulders, hips, knees, and ankles. Match the lower back and stretch slowly and cautiously. Include toe-touching for the hamstrings, but never lock the knees because this puts strain on the lower back and impedes circulation to the calf muscles. Finally, stretch the inner thigh muscles slowly and gently.

Because pregnant women secrete a hormone, *relaxin,* which loosens the pelvic joints in preparation for delivery and also relaxes the tissues surrounding the joints in the rest of the body, Carol advises her students to jog easily on a nice patch of grass or cinder track, and to avoid running on asphalt or cement. Speed and distance are not factors —"Just keep track of the amount of time you spend jogging and keep moving briskly," she tells them, "just keep going for twenty minutes at a conversational pace."

Those women who have sought new levels of self-awareness through running say that going long distances, from ten miles to the marathon, is comparable only to the endurance and ecstasy of childbirth. Others have reached a heightened state of self-awareness by running during pregnancy. Debbie Dewitt took a road tour through Athens, the home of the marathon, in her seventh month—on foot. The Greeks, who weren't used to seeing pregnant women at all, found her a curious figure running up and down hills in her maternity shorts. After getting used to the rough terrain, Debbie fell into a meditative state where "I felt that I was floating, and sensed a real connection with Nature, both inside my body and out. I knew I could go on running for a long, long time."

Getting Started after Forty

While it's easy for a woman in her twenties to run a mile, women in their forties and over deserve special consideration since they tend to be more self-critical when pursuing a new athletic activity and have a lower tolerance of failure. Yet they also have more to gain from a regular running program, including increased self-confidence and self-sufficiency at a time when they're beginning to worry about the vulnerabilities of age.

If you're in that category, just start gradually and run at your slowest pace until you build self-confidence and endurance.

Fifty-eight-year-old Marion Epstein, who got off to a slow start, dodging Brooklyn traffic six years ago when she couldn't run ten blocks, now runs ten miles after work, three nights a week, and then fifteen to eighteen miles on Sunday with her husband, Irving. In the last five years she's racked up twenty-one marathons and shed thirty-seven pounds from her five-foot one-inch frame. "I'm always the last one to finish," laughs Marion, who frequently pulls in a full three hours behind everybody else. "At the Albany Marathon, I was the oldest woman ever in the race. I even did an extra two miles because I got lost!"

Women in their sixties facing early retirement from active professional careers will find that running reinforces their sense of mastery and control and gives them a boost, instilling ego feelings of achievement.

"At first I felt I had one foot on the pavement and another in the grave," says sixty-four-year-old Irene Brown, who was secretary to a college president in Beloit, Wisconsin, when the school choirmaster talked her into jogging. "I didn't seem to be getting anywhere. The wind-chill factor was thirty-five below. And it took me from February to May to do my first mile. Then one of the boys on the Beloit high school track team saw me running and gave me a good lecture about trying to go too fast. The next thing I knew I was running six miles, my appetite had decreased, and I'd lost sixteen pounds."

About that time Irene picked up a magazine for retired executives with a story on athletics for older men. She wrote to them and asked, "Where are your articles for older women?" and sent them a picture of herself running. Irene received a packet of fan mail, mostly from middle-aged women who said they wanted to lose weight and find the sense of freedom as well as the antidote to gloom she ascribed to running.

"I answered every letter and urged them to go slowly and, above all, not to get discouraged. I started most things late in life," she confessed. "I didn't learn to ride a bicycle until I was twenty-five. Now I'm that rare creature—an old woman who runs."

Irene found out just how unsinkable she was, when, as a result of appearing in the magazine, she also received a marriage proposal from a sixty-five-year-old banker. "He said he was looking for an 'old girl' who was active," she recalls, "and we got up at six o'clock to run around the lake. Then we swam, had a few games of tennis, and played bridge. On the second day we ran five and a half miles in forty-eight minutes and spent the rest of the morning climbing the bell tower at the university chapel.

"I don't know if *he* recovered," Irene told me, "but *I'm* still running. I'm not concerned with how fast I can go, though I have done fifteen-mile runs at eight minutes a mile and scaled the backside of Pike's Peak in my hornet green Adidas. Running for me is a time machine. It backs me up and smoothes me out. I feel *reborn*," she crackles, speeding over a quarter-mile dirt track in her mud-speckled shoes.

FOURTEEN

The Primal Run

Three million years ago we stalked the dry savannahs of southern Africa on our newly flattened running feet. The first hominids chased herds of game into canyons and over cliffs, or tirelessly pursued a solitary beast until the animal was exhausted. The Australian aborigine still hunts in this manner, trailing the kangaroo night and day until its muscles grow rigid with fatigue. And the Kalahari bushman runs effortlessly beside the eland for more than twenty miles before moving closer for the kill.

If it weren't for an efficient ball and socket arrangement in the upper thigh, we'd still be picking fruit and scraping nuts off the jungle floor like our predecessors, the vegetarian forest apes. Our nearest competitor in the Pliocene forest was an apelike character called Australopithecus who also walked upright, had binocular vision, and an opposable thumb. But what gave genus Homo a crucial advantage over this imperfectly postured biped was the rotating femur which enabled us to do one thing better: we were natural distance runners.

The question, What makes man man? can be answered by examining our heritage as distance runners. All the qualities we have come to regard as components of "human nature" are direct descendants of our running ways. Early man developed the first syntax of gestures and sounds on these communal runs and evolved a social etiquette as he sat down to share the spoils of the hunt. Because our predatory habits and our running ways are so intertwined, we have begun to look back on our ancestors as killers cast out of Eden for what popular anthropologist Robert Ardrey has called the "original sin": the eating of flesh. Yet what enabled man to hunt was his ability to outrun any land animal. The primary evolutionary characteristic that distinguishes us from the ape, then, is not our aggressive nature or our taste for meat, but the more neutral one of fluid movement, a hypothesis which certainly allows a wider swathe of speculations on the origins of human social habits than a focus on the climax of the kill.

Thaddeus Kostrubala believes that a good deal of human values and behavior is rooted in our running past and that running arouses certain basic inherited characteristics that we are unable to comprehend because of our recent urbanized life-style.

If this is true, then the recent jogging craze is more than just another health fad; it is part of the inbred drive of the species to survive and revive those characteristics that make us more durable to begin with. We may instinctively be running in order to recapture the best and most useful parts of primal man.

Visceral Learning

One of our misconceptions about early man is that he relied more on the faculty of reason and less on a sensory interpretation of the world around him. Yet primitive running man understood the world viscerally, not logically. According to Julian Jaynes, professor of behavioral psychology at Princeton, the fundamental "reasoning" required to fashion crude tools, choose paths and directions, make up words or a syntax of gestures are functions of the nervous system, not of logic or higher consciousness.

In his treatise on bicameral man (primitive man), Jaynes writes: "How often we reach sound conclusions and are quite unable to justify them! Because reasoning is not conscious. Consider the kind of reasoning that we do about other's feelings and character—or in reasoning out the motives of others from their actions. These are clearly the result of automatic inferences by our nervous system . . . consciousness is not only unnecessary but, as we have seen in the performance of motor skills, would probably hinder the process." Thus we begin to see the relative unimportance of consciousness as we know it, and how, in our modern epistemology, we've neglected the tremendous role of body feedback and response.

The tools of primal man's character assessment were biological—they were his eyes, his sense of smell, and perhaps a sort of clairvoyance or telepathy rooted in the nervous system. Running seems to evoke these esoteric physical powers in modern man. Our visual perception, for example, has greatly deteriorated over the span of evolution; the increasing reliance on words as opposed to gestures has resulted in an inability to communicate emotions or basic sensory information through the eyes. Our running ancestors could tell at a glance whether the figure approaching them was friend or foe. But we have a recently acquired gauze over primal vision, which Dr. Elsworth Baker, a Reichian therapist, has labeled "the ocular block." Baker's theory is that once the energy in the body begins to immobilize, this kind of "eyesight" is the first to go. Today many runners report increased confidence in social encounters as a result of their instinctive visceral response and reacting to the visual cues presented "on first sight."

On the run, early man was also aided by his sense of smell, another means of identifying enemies and allies. This is still another sensory vista which explodes when joggers get away from congested traffic or polluted city air. Kostrubala tells of one San Diego runner who delights in the smells of a restaurant three miles off his jogging path. "He runs in an area where the early morning winds blow very lightly and can come from almost any direction," the psychiatrist explains, "including the ocean, which is only half a mile away. It is as if he turned back along the evolutionary trail, fifty thousand, a hundred thousand years, and became ancient man again: the hunter. Out early, his senses alert, his blood powerfully flowing, the pores of his skin open, his eyes clear. And the most primitive sense organ—the sense of smell—is triggered."

Freud was the first one to suggest that telepathy may have been the original archaic method by which individuals understood one another. And people who run together frequently experience a kind of synchronous bonding, based on the shared revolutions of the run. As they move together, the air between them becomes a viscous medium for the nonverbal transmission of their thoughts. Psychiatrist Kostrubala believes that running therapy creates an entirely new kind of bond between therapist and patient—one based on the shared visceral sensations of the run. "It's like dreaming the same dream as the patient at the same time," he explains. Similarly, jogging companions will report having identical images pop into their minds during their daily runs. A doctor running along the cliffs in Del Mar, California, envisioned a long procession of joggers carrying torches up the beach. When later in the week he told his friend the details of his dreamlike vision, the other man interrupted, "But I imagined the same event—*exactly*—on my run!"

Our running ancestors were also adept at "energy sensing"—being able to tell whether an aggressive or hostile force was approaching from behind. This is a technique that George Leonard, author of *The Ultimate Athlete,* has incorporated into his aikido classes in Mill Valley. After one of his classes at the aikido dojo, we ran through the wooded trails on Mount Tamalpais, with two of his colleagues. As we cut through the narrow paths, I was acutely aware of George, Leo, and Susan running behind me, as though I could sense their reactions to a newcomer in the group and feel their unspoken intentions leaving a fine impression on the photographic "energy plate" of my mind.

When primitive man got into unfriendly situations or encountered circumstances he couldn't handle, he may have heard "voices" telling him what to do. According to psychologist Julian Jaynes, these auditory hallucinations were created by the nervous system; but early man took them to be "gods" giving him instructions on how to act under duress. In so many words, our ancestors were prone to a certain kind of behavior, such as hearing *warning* "voices" and acting on their commands, that today would be diagnosed as schizophrenic.

But schizophrenia may actually be an adaptive behavior of early running man to the stress and isolation of the hunt. The intuition of conspiracies in paranoid schizophrenics may be a throwback to primitive times where man's life depended on his advance detection of danger. These suspicions are a function of the right hemisphere of the brain which is also responsible for nonverbal processing of sensory information. The left side of the brain, which specializes in linear, logical, and analytic thought developed much later.

Like sudden bursts of creative insight that release adrenaline in the body and are accompanied by mild physical shock, all knowledge came to our running ancestors in biological form. According to recent brain research, most of the mind is concerned with muscle functions, while only a small percentage is occupied with "consciousness" as we now know it. Hence we learn things quicker if we absorb them physically—through muscles and through movement—and then transmit this knowledge to the conscious brain. This is the basis for one of the axioms of behavioral psychology: learning is more effective when accompanied by physical trauma, or that ideas are retained longer when absorbed during intense activity. Anthropologist Gregory Bateson sums it up more poetically. "The way we think is a consequence of our biology," he says, and adds that anyone who perceives a theoretical problem with his entire system, filtering the question through the senses *and* the mind, will be quicker to find a solution than someone who approaches the subject only with his intellect. This is because all relationships can be reduced to a common denominator: "All living things have a grammar and a syntax analogous to our own." In all of nature, there is only one basic plot, the pattern of contraction and expansion, of arousal and release, that we experience within the context of our nervous system in the microcosm of the run.

If you've ever met an excruciating pedant and found yourself unable to extract one whole concept from his fabric of detail, you might suggest, politely, that he take up running and reestablish himself in the physical world. If he cannot see the forest for the trees, it's because he has forgotten that the smallest forms of life contain essentially the same "information" and operate according to the same pulsing rhythms as we do.

In the sixth century B.C. the Pythagoreans practiced a firm illiteracy. They considered it a mistake to write things down because they felt learning should involve the whole man and not just the part of him that could sort, analyze, and store information. They knew that any conscious discovery had an analogue in the body and would be accompanied, at the very least, by a grunt and gasp of recognition, if not a sudden sprint around the room (occasioned by the release of some adrenaline). I recently overheard two marathoners—one a respected lawyer and the other a real estate executive—discussing the body-mind dilemma, like Pythagoreans in modern garb. "If you had to make a choice," one said to the other, "which would you give up—running or reading?"

Just how much movement is a part of the learning experience is revealed in the structure of our language. The most elementary syntax takes its shape from the idea of a physical journey. And running is the primal metaphor for the way we think and communicate. It is representative of the larger journey of our lifetime, and still so much a part of our everyday consciousness that we project it onto objective measures of time and space (clock and trains "run" according to schedules), our emotional state (we "run away" from difficult relationships), or work life (we "run" governments, armies, companies, and banks), and our ideas of success (people who "get ahead" are those who can "go the distance"). Since the *Iliad,* poets have invoked the same metaphors of pounding hearts and breathless anticipation to describe the horrors of battle—and the arousal of true love. In fact, there are more definitions and derivative uses of "run" in Webster's than for any other word in the English language.

A Return to the Values of the Run

"Every Sunday we take an eight-mile hike—run from the beach at Palos Verdes to the high point on the peninsula. Each of us carries a small pebble from the ocean up a 2,000-

foot cliff. We leave them at the foot of a large boulder, a sort of altar rock. It's an experiment in time: every runner knows that it will take 15 million years for his pebble to get back to the sea," says T. J. Bass, a science fiction writer who belongs to the Seniors Track Club in Palos Verdes, California. His group, like many others, has evolved a ritual around their weekly run. Bass describes it with almost religious awe: "My little rock is nothing. It's just a symptom of what takes place as life unfolds: we came out of the ocean and up on land for a reason. We have a purpose in our genes and our genes are made from atoms. Who knows —maybe there's a little spiritual push in every atom."

The feeling that each life matters and that every one of us is in direct communication with some greater force is also a holdover from our primal running days. Early man spent more time on religion than anything else, and for him running was not only the means by which he made his living but a ritual way of storing up energy. He knew the power he invested in the run would come back to him in terms of increased strength and endurance. And his religion was securely grounded in the revolutions of his body on the long hunting journeys, his first cosmology rooted in the rhythms of the run.

Now a San Diego group holds *tesquinadas,* long runs through the Torrey pines patterned on the sacred running games of the Tarahumara Indians of northern Mexico. And in La Jolla a small tribe runs along the beach at nightfall, carrying lighted torches in a pagan celebration of the summer solstice.

In *The Hunting Hypothesis,* Robert Ardrey calls our attention to "two psychic qualities which pervade us all, regardless of our literacy or sophistication. The first is an inner need to believe in forces larger and more enduring than oneself. And the second is the illusion of central posi-

tion (that man is the focus of the universe). Both are in-
eradicable legacies of our hunting days." He goes on to say
that the social isolation of the hunt reinforced the notion
that each tribe was the inheritor of the earth. Primitive man
could run for miles without encountering another soul. But
when we left the hunt for an agrarian existence, we were
thrown into a world of strangers, for which we were biologically unprepared.

It's not surprising, therefore, that running is often an
"urban cure." One New York woman described her need to
run as an antidote to the oppressive crowding and narrow
space allotments—windowless office and studio apartment
—in the city. "Running gives me back my own feelings of
body-space and allows me to expand my territory, to stretch
my physical world beyond its normal tight enclosures, she
explained. And a Chicago runner said she felt herself become tight, compact, as though she would consolidate herself against the waves of noise, pollution, and pushing
crowds. Clearly jogging is a way of staking out a territorial
claim. One that begins with the right to our own bodies and
encompasses ancestral lands that we inherit in the run.

We also shed a veneer of urban self-consciousness and
come back to the core of what we share with other living
things. Running restores us to the natural tides of body time
and body space, allowing us to transcend the cramped
existence between trains and buses and crackerbox walls,
and to enter the larger biological realm, where we begin to
understand the process of renewal and decay.

The awareness of our temporary tenure here on earth
creeps poignantly into an occasional run and deepens our
appreciation of this life. It comes as a thick, sensuous feeling
of being wrapped in a body that is part of the continuously
changing fund of matter, of sticks and stones, flesh and
bones. Or as a piercing melancholy that illuminates the

edges of existence, described by poet Roger Eischens in *Run to Reality:*

> *Running*
> *talking of the fear of dying*
> *and the sudden and continuing realization*
> *that my friends and I will soon be gone*
> *Even the earth is temporary*
> *My friend is drained by the burden*
> *of looking death in the eye*
> *Having experienced his mortality so clearly*
> *he can never fool himself again.*
> *He talks of feeling alone*
> *of wanting to relate closely*
> *about energy ties between friends*
> *the importance of community*
> *ties to the life energy of the earth*
> *Reality grows . . .*
> *A glimpse caught of death*
> *A realization of intimacy*
> *We run on*
> *Lengthening the time of our closeness.*

Aristotle once wrote that nature is like a runner, in that it goes from being to nonbeing and back. In the psychic process of the run we experience our own mortality in every step, in every breath; we commit ourselves to the distance, to the irreversible destinies of our lives. We see our values and accomplishments from the other side, like the Greek god Hermes, the runner who carried souls to the Underworld and was able to come back. Then "reality grows" and we begin the process of renewal and return.

On a hot spring day a small group of us ran along a deserted stretch of New York's West Side Highway past the piers and sewage plants and old, abandoned warehouses. I suddenly had the feeling, looking at the skyline through the rising heat, that in time all of this would be gone. In my science fiction fantasy we were running through the rubble of a dying civilization. Our tiny group would be the sole survivors; we were durable, strong, like primal running man. And we had the benefits of three million years of developing consciousness.

But this fictional scenario may not be so distant from the truth. Historian William Irwin Thompson predicts a retribalization of society and a breakdown into hunter-gatherer-sized groups by the year 2000. This will be accompanied as well by an "interiorization" of consciousness. People will once again look within for the good life, rather than without. They will depend on their own ingenuity rather than a vast industrial network, and will form a community based on the self-sufficiency of the run: where simplicity is a blessing and economy an art.

The seeds of this transformation already lie in small tribes of people meditating and running through the California forests, the lakelands of Wisconsin, in Zen monasteries in the Northeast, and through the labyrinthian concrete of New York City streets. These individuals are exploring the body as the touchstone to awakening consciousness in a new holistic age and discovering primordial truths about the way human beings operate through running. These include a reactivation of the archaic parts of the brain responsible for sensory and extrasensory perception; a return to the concept of the Earth as a nurturing, supportive force; a reverence for the mysteries of creation, and an understanding of irreversible biological time; and a reestablishment of our need for ritual, for a way to celebrate our individuality and restore a sense of personal power and mastery over our environment.

The runner's life-style is unique, and people do change once they begin to run regularly. First comes the unconscious alteration of the diet, the natural fasting before the run. Then a paring down of material needs. An increased sense of intimacy and sharing with special friends. A weeding out of superfluous people. A growing sense of strength and endurance that translates into self-confidence and builds to a religious awe of man *in* nature. Whatever your religion, you will become more *it*. Because suddenly you will begin to see the mysteries of creation all around you in the run.

For over three million years Nature has preserved the most valuable components of the primal run pressed into the narrow-ribboned chromosomes of genetic necessity. What *is* our ancient ability to run long distances, what psychological states and psychic powers does it evoke? We may find the answer in the sweat and heat of the marathon, or on the jogger's path. However far we go, the mysteries are within us, ready to be revealed; we are running reborn along the evolutionary trail.

Bibliography

ARDREY, ROBERT, *The Hunting Hypothesis,* New York: Atheneum, 1976.

ARTAUD, ANTONIN, "A Voyage to the Land of the Tarahumara," *The Peyote Dance,* New York, Farrar, Straus and Giroux, 1976.

BAKER, ELSWORTH, *Man in the Trap,* New York: Macmillan, 1967.

BASSLER, THOMAS J., "Marathon Running and Immunity to Athersclerosis," *Annals of the New York Academy of Sciences,* Vol. 301, 1977, pp. 579–593.

BENTOV, ITZHAK, *Stalking the Wild Pendulum: On the Mechanics of Consciousness,* New York: Dutton, 1976.

BROWN, BARBARA, *New Mind, New Body,* New York: Harper & Row, 1974.

BUDZYNSKI, THOMAS, "Turning in on the Twilight Zone," *Psychology Today,* August, 1977, pp. 38–44.

CAPRA, FRITJOF, *The Tao of Physics,* New York: Bantam Books, 1977.

COOPER, KENNETH, *Aerobics,* New York: Bantam Books, 1968.

DAVID-NEEL, ALEXANDRA, "Psychic Sports, Mystic Theories and Spiritual Training," *Magic and Mystery in Tibet,* New York: Dover, 1971.

191

DEWEY, EDWARD, AND MANDINO, OG, *Cycles, The Mysterious Forces That Trigger Events,* New York: Hawthorn, 1971.

DICARA, LEO, "Learning in the Autonomic Nervous System," *Scientific American,* January, 1970, pp. 30–39.

DILFER, CAROL, *Your Baby, Your Body: Fitness During Pregnancy,* New York: Crown, 1977.

DODSON, O. C., AND MULLENS, W. R., "Some Effects of Jogging on Psychiatric Hospital Patients," *American Corrective Therapy Journal,* 23 (5): 130–134, 1969.

DRISCOLL, R., "Anxiety Reduction Using Physical Exertion and Positive Images," *Psychological Record,* 26, 87–94, 1976.

ECCLES, JOHN C., "The Physiology of Imagination," *Scientific American,* September, 1958, pp. 135–142.

FELDENKRAIS, MOSHE, *Awareness Through Movement,* New York: Harper & Row, 1972.

FIXX, JAMES, *The Complete Book of Running,* New York: Random House, 1977.

GLASSER, WILLIAM, *Positive Addiction,* New York: Harper & Row, 1976.

GREIST, JOHN, AND EISCHENS, ROGER, *Run to Reality,* Milwaukee: Bulfin, 1977.

GUTHRIE, D., AND GARY, V., "The Effect of Jogging on Physical Fitness and Self-Concept in Hospitalized Alcoholics," *Quarterly Journal for the Study of Alcohol,* 33: 1073–1078, 1972.

GUTIN, B., "The Effect of Increase in Physical Fitness on Mental Ability Following Physical and Mental Stress," *Research Quarterly,* 37: 211–220, 1966.

HARRIS, DOROTHY V., AND JENNINGS, SUSAN E., "Self-Perceptions of Female Distance Runners," *Annals of the New York Academy of Sciences,* Vol. 301, 1977, pp. 808–816.

HEISENBERG, WERNER, *Physics and Philosophy: The Revolution in Modern Science,* New York: Harper & Row, 1958.

HERON, WOODBURN, "The Pathology of Boredom," *Scientific American,* January, 1957, pp. 52–56.

ISMAIL, A. H., AND TRACHTMAN, L. E., "Jogging the Imagination," *Psychology Today,* March, 1973, pp. 79–82.

JAMES, WILLIAM, *The Varieties of Religious Experience,* New York: New American Library, 1958.

JAYNES, JULIAN, *The Origin of Consciousness in the Breakdown of the Bicameral Mind,* Boston: Houghton Mifflin, 1977.

JONAS, GERALD, *Visceral Learning,* New York: Viking 1973.

JOUVET, MICHAEL, "The States of Sleep," *Scientific American,* February, 1967, pp. 62–68.

KERENYI, KARL, *Hermes: Guide of Souls,* Zurich: Spring Publications, 1976.

KLEITMAN, NATHANIEL, "Patterns of Dreaming," *Scientific American,* November, 1960, pp. 82–88.

KOSTRUBALA, THADDEUS, *The Joy of Running,* Philadelphia: Lippincott, 1976.

KUSCSIK, NINA, "The History of Women's Participation in the Marathon," *Annals of the New York Academy of Sciences,* Vol. 301, 1977, pp. 862–877.

LANCE, KATHERYN, *Running for Health and Beauty,* New York: Bobbs-Merrill, 1976.

LEONARD, GEORGE, *The Ultimate Athlete,* New York: Viking, 1974.

LE SHAN, LAWRENCE, *Alternate Realities,* New York: M. Evans, 1976.

————, *How to Meditate,* Boston: Little, Brown, 1974.

————, *The Medium, the Mystic and the Physicist,* New York: Viking, 1975.

LOWEN, ALEXANDER, *Pleasure,* New York: Coward-McCann, 1970.

LUCE, GAY GAER, *Body Time,* New York: Random House, 1971.

MILVY, PAUL, ed., "The Marathon: Physiological, Medical, Epidemiological, and Psychological Studies," *Annals of the New York Academy of Sciences,* Vol. 301, New York, 1977.

MULLER, B., AND ARMSTRONG, H. E., "A Further Note on the Running Treatment for Anxiety," *Psychotherapy: Theory, Research, and Practice,* 12 (4): 385–387, 1975.

MURPHY, MICHAEL, *Jacob Atabet: A Speculative Fiction,* Millbrae, California: Celestial Arts, 1977.

ORNSTEIN, ROBERT E., *On the Experience of Time,* New York: Penguin, 1969.

————, *The Psychology of Consciousness,* New York: Penguin, 1972.

ORWIN, ARNOLD, "The Running Treatment, A Preliminary Communication of a New Use for an Old Therapy (Physical Activity) in the Agoraphobic Syndrome," *British Journal of Psychiatry,* 122: 175–179, 1973.

————, "Treatment of a Situational Phobia—A Case for Running," *British Journal of Psychiatry,* 125: 95–98, 1974.

OYLE, IRVING, *The Healing Mind,* Millbrae, California: Celestial Arts, 1975.

PIAGET, JEAN, *The Child's Conception of Movement and Speed,* New York: Ballantine, 1971.

PLATO, *Timaeus,* tr. Desmond Lee, London: Cox & Wyman, 1965.

PROGOFF, IRA, *At a Journal Workshop,* New York: Dialogue House Library, 1975.

SAGAN, CARL, *The Dragons of Eden, Speculations on the Evolution of Human Intelligence,* New York: Random House, 1977.

SHAINBERG, DAVID, "Long Distance Running as Meditation," *Annals of the New York Academy of Sciences,* Vol. 301, 1977, pp. 1002–1010.

SHEEHAN, GEORGE, *Dr. Sheehan on Running,* Mountain View, California: World Publications, 1975.

SPINO, MICHAEL, *Beyond Jogging—The Innerspaces of Running,* Millbrae, California: Celestial Arts, 1975.

————, *Running Home: The Body/Mind Family Fitness Book,* Millbrae, California: Celestial Arts, 1977.

SUZUKI, SHUNRYU, *Zen Mind, Beginner's Mind,* New York: Weatherhill, 1970.

THOMAS, LEWIS, *The Lives of a Cell,* New York: Viking, 1974.

THOMPSON, WILLIAM IRWIN, *At the Edge of History,* New York: Harper & Row, 1971.

ULLYOT, JOAN, *Women's Running,* Mountain View, California: Runner's World, 1976.

WALLACE, ROBERT KEITH, AND BENSON, HERBERT, "The Physiology of Meditation," *Scientific American,* February, 1972, pp. 84–90.

Index

Aborigine, Australian, 179
Accomplishment, 38
Achilles tendon, 66
Action, 43
  thought and, 9–10, 148
Addictions, 63
  negative. *See* Negative addictions
  positive, 53, 56, 102
Addicts, self-criticism of, 52–53
Adolescents, 11
Adrenaline, 38, 44
  "fight or flight" response and, 44–45
Aerobics (Cooper), 174
Age
  pulse rates and, 26–27
  women over forty, 176–78
  See also Aging
Agency (masculine instinct), 164
Aggression (aggressiveness), 33, 65, 79
  heart disease and, 62
  of men, 164
Aging
  of Achilles tendon, 66
  premature, 59, 67
Agoraphobics, 46
Aikido, 4, 96, 111–12, 183
Alcohol (alcoholism, alcoholics), 25, 35, 51–54, 62
  heart disease and, 63, 64
Alienation
  from body, 8, 20, 23
  from nature, 98, 136
Altered states of consciousness, 4, 6, 56, 83, 96, 100–3
  electromagnetic fields and, 136
  Esalen and, 113
Amateur Athletic Union, 158–61
American Medical Jogging Association, 62, 66

Androgeny
  of mind and body, 7
  women and, 158, 164–66
Anger, 13, 19, 38, 171
  self-directed, 41–43
Ankles, 31
Anxiety, 5, 8, 33, 35, 51, 68
  breathlessness and, 45–47
  confrontation of, through running, 49–50
  dreams and, 84
  "fight or flight" response to, 44–45
  military reaction to, 44
  trusting your body and control of, 47–49
Appetite, 84
Appointments, with friends, 40–41
Archery, 101
Archetypal unconscious, 83
  See also Collective unconscious
Archetypes (archetypal experiences), 79, 136
  decoding of, 92–95
Ardrey, Robert, 180, 186–87
Aristotle, 184, 188
Arms, 28
Armstrong, Hubert, 46–47
Artaud, Antonin, 130–31
Arteries, aging of, 66
Arteriosclerosis, 63, 65
Asceticism, 101
  See also Mystics; Tibetan monks
Australian Aborigine, 179

Baekeland, Frederick, 8
Baker, Elsworth, 181
Balanese rituals, 44
Bantu warriors, 65
Bass, T. J., 186
Bassler, Thomas, 62, 64

Bateson, Gregory, 184
Beginner's mind, 103, 105–6
Bell, Jess, 142
Benton, Janice, 171
Bentov, Itzhak, 135, 138
Berman, Sara Mae, 159
Beyond Jogging: The Inner-spaces of Running (Murphy), 113–14
Biological process, the run as, 11
Biorhythmic cycles, 59–61
Blood pressure, control of, 123
Bloodstream, epinephrine in, 34
Body
    alienation from, 8, 20, 23
    fear and trusting your, 47–49
    women's attitudes about, 172–73
    See also specific topics
Body and mind, 9–10, 133
    androgyny of, 7
    dialogue of, 14–25
    entrainment of, 87
    synchronicity of, 11–14
    transformation of, 6, 112
Body awareness, 89–91
Body density meditation, 119
Body-image, 15
Bohm, David, 135
Bonne Bell, 142
Boston Marathon, 158, 160–61
Brain (brain power), 183, 184
    increase in, 153–54
Breathing (breath), 9, 13, 29, 52, 54, 57
    control of, 123
Breathlessness, 5, 45
Brodie, John, 111
Brown, Irene, 177–78
Buddha, 101
Businessmen, 141–42

Caffeine, 25
California, 68
Calories, 65
Cancer, 124–25
Carbohydrates, 60, 65
Cardiovascular activity, 45

Cardiac output, target rates for, 26–27
Careers (jobs, work), 29, 38
    changes in, 72–73
    energy for, 69–70
    See also Success
Cassini, Oleg, 145
Center for Cancer Counseling Research, 125
Cerutty, Percy, 112, 115
Chandler, Tom, 61
Chanting, 81
    See also Mantras
Character-building, 52
Chase Manhattan Bank, 146
Childbirth, marathons compared to, 176
Childhood, memories of, 13–14
Children, 11, 22
China, 62
Chinmoy, Sri, 99–100, 139
Cholesterol, 62, 65
Cierpinski, Waldemar, 122
Cigarettes (smoking), 25, 26, 51, 52, 62
    heart disease and, 63, 64
Circle-running, 44
Circulation, 4, 34, 52, 65
Clay, Jim, 149
Clinics, 36, 70, 72
Clothes, 31
Cold, 34
Collective unconscious, 79, 83, 85
    synchronous bonding and, 138–40
Colors, 82
Colt, Edward, 34
Commitment, 144
Communion (feminine instinct), 164
Competence, 38
Competition, 7, 37, 81
    fear of, 89–91
    women and, 167–69
Compulsive personalities, 10–11
    See also Type A personalities
Concentration, 6, 37
Connective tissues, 32, 65, 66

Consciousness
altered states of, *see* Altered
states of consciousness
levels of, 136–38
survival and, 100
synchronization of, 138–40
transcending the boundaries
of, 101
Control, 7, 34, 49–50, 63, 123,
177
of anxiety, 45
of breathing, 29
fear of loss of, 11
of heart, 123–24
of time, 70
Cool-downs, 29, 30
Cooper, Kenneth, 144, 174
Corporations, employees of,
141–42
Cosmology
Greek, 133–135, 140
modern, 135–38
movement and the collective
mind, 138–40
of Tarahumara Indians, 130–
31
See also Universe
Cotton, 31
Counting, 81
Cox, Terry, 171–72
Cramps, 16, 31, 32, 54
Crane, Harriet, 37
Creativity, 6, 73, 148
Heller on, 151–52
Russell on, 151
tension and, 155–56
Crisis, 13
Crowe, Peter, 48
Cycles, 5
biorhythmic, 59–61
of depression, 38
dream, 84
See also Rhythms

Dancing (dances), 44, 110
of All the Night, 131
disco, 57
Greek, 134
Darius I, 44

Dating. *See* Social life
Death, fear of, 47
Deep breathing, 57
Dependency, 8, 9, 164
Depression, 33–43, 73, 74
biochemical basis of, 33–35
draining off negative emotions
and, 41–43
Greist's program and, 39–40
postpartum, 174
sedentary life-style and, 35–41
Dewey, Edward, 61
Dewitt, Debbie, 176
Dialogue
between body and mind, 14–
35
with mental mentors, 153
Diary, *see* Journal
Diet, 26, 32, 62, 63
prevention, 65
Dienstbier, Richard, 34
Dilfer, Carol, 173–76
Disco dancing, 57
Discrimination, against women,
158–61
Divorce. *See* Marital problems
Donaldson, Brenda, 162–63
Doors of Perception, The
(Huxley), 100–1
Dream(s), 5, 79, 83–95, 153
collective unconscious and, 85
curtailment of, 84
decoding of, 92–95
healing and, 84–85
journal record of, 88–91
Kostrubala's most memorable,
87–88
in Senoi culture, 93–94
stress and, 87
Drives, *see* Instincts
Drugs, 43, 51, 52, 77

Eastern disciplines, 4, 96, 101
See also Meditation; Zen-like
states or experiences
Eating (food), 5, 25, 51, 52, 60
See also Diet; Overeating
Eccles, John, 150–51
Ego, the, 137, 138

Egypt, 6
Eischens, Roger, 98, 188
Electromagnetic fields, 135–36
Elite, runners as, 111–12
Elliot, Herb, 112
Emerson, Ralph Waldo, 144,
    151
Emotions, 4, 29, 33, 106
    body feelings and, 11
    hidden, 76, 82–83
    honesty about, 12–13
"Enantiodrama," 93
Endurance
    building of, 117–18
    speed and, 28–29
    women and, 159–60
End-watching, 103–6
Energy, 69, 73, 136
"Energy sensing," 183
Entrainment, 87, 139–40
Epinephtine, 34
Epstein, Marion, 177
Esalen
    founding of, 113
    meditation and mental im-
        agery program of, 119–22
    training program of, 114–19
Escape, anxiety and, 46
ESP (extrasensory perception),
    140
Euphoria ("runner's high"), 34,
    51, 57, 58, 97, 102
    psychotherapy and, 82
Evolution, 88
    genetic information for, 136,
        137
    of psyche, 78–79
Exercises
    meditation, 107–110, 119–22,
        125–28
    for pregnant women, 174–76
    warm-up, 29–30, 64
Executives, business, 141–42
Exhaling, 50
Exhaustion, nervous, 37
Extrasensory communication,
    140
Eyes, 181

Falling, fear of, 93–94
Fatigue (tiredness), 29, 35, 38,
    119, 121
Fear(s), 5, 44–50
    of abandonment, 11–12
    breathlessness and, 45–47
    of competition, 89, 90, 91
    confrontation of, 49–50
    dreams and freedom from,
        93–95
    of falling, 93–94
    "fight or flight" response to,
        44–45, 94–95
    trusting your body and control
        of, 47–49
Feelings, body, emotions and, 11
Females. *see* Women
Femininity, stereotypes of, 164
Femur, rotating, 7, 59, 179
Fetscher, Paul, 145–46
"Fight or flight" response, 44–
    45, 94–95
Fitness, optimum level of, 6
Fluid exchange, 34
Finnerty, Sue, 170–71
Food (eating), 5, 25, 51, 52, 60
    See also Diet; Overeating
Foot, 28, 31
Form, 27–28
Forster, E. M., 35
Foundation for the Study of
    Cycles, 61
Fresh swing, 115–18
Friends, appointments with, 40–
    41
Freud, Sigmund
    the psyche and, 136
    on telepathy, 182

Gallway, Timothy, 4
Gas, stomach, 15, 32
Genetic traits, 136, 137
Gilmore, Ken, 155–56
Glasser, William, 51–53, 56, 57,
    102
Glycogen fuels, 98
Glucose, 33
Goethe, Johann Wolfgang von,
    105

Goals, 22–23, 52, 53, 142
    choice of, 167
    incentive and maintenance, 7,
        146
    See also End-watching
Gontang, Austin, 12, 13
Good swing, 115, 117–18
Gordon, Mary, 146
Greeks (Greece), 3, 6, 33
    cosmology of, 133–35, 140
    dances of, 134
    dreams and, 85
    at Marathon, 44
Greist, John, 35, 36, 47
    training program of, 39–40
Groaning, 156
Group(s)
    psychic identity of, 138–40
    running in, 6

Habits, *see* Addictions
Hallucinations, 79, 183
Hamstrings, 30, 31
Happiness, 70
Harnad, John, 154
Harris, Dorothy, 164, 165
Haynes, Phyllis, 98
Headlands Healing Service, 131
Head rolls, 30
Healing (cures), 6, 52
    among Tarahumara Indians,
        130–31
    dreams and, 84
    loneliness and, 36
    meditations for, 125–30
Heart, 5, 9
    control of, 123–24
Heart disease
    arteriosclerosis, 63, 65
    marathoners with, 124
    prevention diet for, 65
    sedentary life-style and, 61–62
    "Type A" personalities and,
        62–63
Heel, 28
Heller, Joseph, 151–52
Hellerstein, Herman, 63
Helplessness, 11–12

Herodotus, 44
Heroism, 99
Hirsch, George, 147
Holographic model of the uni-
    verse, 135–38
Honesty, 12–13
Hormones. *See* Testosterone
Hostility, 38
    self-directed, 41–43
    See also Aggression; Anger
Hubbard, Fred, 37
Humor, 106
Hunting Hypothesis, The
    (Ardrey), 186–87
Hutchins, Robert Maynard, 67–
    68
Huxley, Aldous, 100–101
Hypertension, 35, 65
Hypochondria, 46

Igloi, Mihaly, 115
Imagery. *See* Dream(s); Visuali-
    zation(s)
Imagination, 148
    Eccles on, 150–51
Immune system, 6
Incentive goals, 7, 146
Independence, 9, 70, 164
    See also Self-confidence
Individuality, 52
Infection, yeast, 31
Inhibitions. *See* Psychological
    barriers; Resistance(s)
Injuries, 57–58, 64
Inner games, 4, 96
Insecurities, 11
Instincts (drives), 7, 45, 68
    female and male, 164–65
Integration, of personality, 5, 84
Intellectual life, 10, 99, 104
Interval training, 115–19
Intimacy, 70
Introspection, 6, 36
Intuition, 104, 111
Irritability, 84
Ismail, A. H., 33, 34, 65
Isolation, social, 171
IUD (intrauterine device), 166

James, William, 96, 154
  on success, 167
Jaw, 30
Jaynes, Julian, 180–81, 183
Jensen, Jim, 150
Jerome, Saint, 101
Jobs. *See* Careers; Work
"Jogging for Jobs," 142
"Jogger's toe," 31
Journal (diary, log), 40, 146
  accounting system of, 145
  dream records, 83, 88–91
  therapeutic run entries, 24–25
Joy of Running, The (Kostru-
  bala), 71
Jung, Carl G., 79, 136
  dreams and, 85
  on "enantiodrama," 93

Kalahari bushmen, 60
Kamen, Jeff, 139
Karate, 4
Knees, 121
Koenig, Stephanie, 166
Kostrubala, Thaddeus, 68–72,
  74–77, 180, 182
  dream of, 87–88
  Paleoanalytic Psychology of,
  78–79, 81, 88
  on resonating with the un-
  conscious, 82–83
Kramer, Larry, 155
Kravitz, Sara, 149
Kuscsik, Nin, 158–59, 161, 164

Lactic acid, 29
Landy, John, 112
Learning
  suggestive, 150
  trauma and, 184
  visceral, 180–85
Leonard, George, 67–68, 111,
  183
Lewis, Larry, 66
Life-expectancy, 62, 66–68
Life-style changes, 4, 5, 71
  See also Social life
Log, *see* Journal
Loneliness, 36

Longevity Institute (Los Angeles), 65
"Love and Serve" runs, 99
Lung Gom Pa (Tibetan monks),
  106, 113

McGrath, Ellie, 168
MacKenzie, Christine, 160
MacKenzie, Marlin, 14
MacLaine, Shirley, 143
Maintenance goals, 7, 146
Man as hunter, 186–87
Man as runner, 179–90
  return to primal values, 185–
  90
  visceral learning, 180–85
Manic-depressives, 34
Mantras, 81, 149
Marathon(s)
  Boston, 158, 160–61
  businessmen in, 145–47
  cancer patient in, 125
  cardiac patients in, 124–25
  childbirth compared to, 176
  heroism and, 98, 99
  Maryland, 166
  meaning and, 157
  New York City, 161
  on Pike's Peak, 159
  women in, 168–69
Marathoners
  socio-economic status of, 141
  See also specific individuals
Marital problems, 54–55, 73–76,
  85–86
Martial arts, 96, 101
Martial music, 149
Masai warriers, 65
Masculinity, stereotypes of, 164
Mastery (self-mastery), 7, 49,
  177
Materialism (material security),
  73–74
Meditation(s), 6, 56, 96–110,
  119–22
  Chinmoy and, 99
  end-watching and, 103–6
  healing, 125–30
  how to reach state of, 106–7

Meditation(s) (*continued*)
  physiology of, 100–3
  "Safe Harbor," 107
  sensory awareness, 107–10
  Dyveke Spino's, 108–10, 128–30
  Tibetan log, 107
Meggesey, Dave, 111
Melpomene, 158
Memorex, 142
Memory(-ies)
  of childhood, 13–14
  imagination and, 150–51
Menstruation, 16
Mental imagery. *See* Visualization(s)
Mental mentors, 153
Merrill, Robert, 143, 150
Metabolism, change of, 114, 115
Meyer, Fred, 142
Miller, Bart, 46–47
Mill Valley Physical Therapy Center, 107
Mind
  beginner's, 103, 105–6
  collective, synchronous bonding and, 138–40
  See also Consciousness; Psyche, the; Unconscious, the
Mind and body. *See* Body and mind
Mind at Large, 100–101
Montague, Ashley, 59, 67
Moore, Kathy, 70
Morale, corporate, 142
Morphine derivative, 52
Motivation, 165
Motor development, 11–12
Murphy, Michael, 98, 112–13
Muscles, 4, 8, 21, 30, 32, 33, 121
  anxiety and, 45
  dissociation from, 20
  leg, 66
  stomach, 28
  the will as, 145–46
Muscle fatigue, 35
Myerson, Bess, 150

Mystics, 6, 96, 101
Mystery schools, 6
Mythology, personal, 5, 92

Napping, 60
Narrative, natural, 9
Nature
  alienation from, 98
  religion and, 96
Negative addictions, 51
  relationships as, 54–55
  self-criticism and, 52–54
Nervous exhaustion, 37
New Times (magazine), 147
New York City marathon, 161
Nightmares. *See* Dreams
Nonverbal communication, 140

Olympic games
  of 1896, 158
  Greek, 3
Orwin, Arnold, 45
Out-of-body states, 6, 111, 121
Overeating (obesity), 53, 62, 63, 64
  See also Weight problems
Overthink, 154–55
Overwork, 154–55
Oxygen flow (oxygen utilization), 4, 35, 65
Oyle, Irving, 132

Pain (soreness), 17, 23, 39, 40, 54, 155
  dreams and, 84–85
  menstrual, 16
  psychosomatic, 11, 12, 24, 35, 84–85
  tranquilizers, 42–43
Paleoanalytic Psychology, 78–79, 81, 88
Panic, 45
Paradise, Laverne, 166
Parks, Emma, 40
Passivity, 164
Patience, 38
Peachtree Center, 143
Pearson, Richard, 34

Perception changes, 82, 97, 100, 181
Perfect runner, image of, 120–21
Period cramps, 16
Persians, 44
Personality (personality changes, personality traits), 7, 34, 68–71
    careers and, 72–73
    compulsive, 10–11
    integration of, 5, 84
    marriage and, 73–76
    Type A, 62–64
    of women, 7, 164–66
Phobia, *see* Agoraphobics; Fear
Physical changes
    biorhythmic cycles, reestablishment of, 60–61
    heart disease prevention, 62–65
    life-expectancy increases, 62, 66–68
Physical examination, 26
Physiology of meditation, 100–3
Pieper, Arlene, 159
Plato, 10, 133–35, 140
Portman, John, 143
Postpartum depression, 174
Powerlessness, 5, 35, 43
Prayer, 70, 97
Pregnancy, 173–76
Prenatal and Postpartum Aerobic Fitness Program, 174–75
Prevention diet, 65
Primal run, 148
Primitive man, 44, 60, 186–97, 179–90
Prinze, Rosalie, 169–70
Pritikin, Nathan, 65
Problem-solving (problem-solving ability), 7, 73, 97, 142
    unconscious, 151–55
Protein, 65
Psyche(s)
    Freud's concept of, 136
    levels of, 136–38

Psyche(s) (*continued*)
    Paleoanalytic model of, 78–79, 81, 88
    synchronous bonding of, 138
Psychological barriers, of women, 161–64
Psychosclerosis, 59
Psychosis, 34
Psychosomatic ailments, 11, 12, 24, 35
    dreams and, 84–85
Psychotherapy (therapy), 35–36, 69, 170
    body-mind synchronicity and, 14–35
    jogging as tool in, 14–25
    "runner's high" and, 82
Pulse, 26–27
Purification, 52
Push-ups, vertical, 30
Pythagoreans, 184–85

Rationality (reason), 99, 104, 180–81
Rebirth, 6, 69, 98, 99
    Balanese ceremony for, 44
Reich, Wilhelm, 11
Relationships, 5, 8, 29, 38, 70
    anger about, 41–43
    destructive, 54–55, 75
    marital problems, 54–55, 73–76, 85–86
    the unconscious and, 76
    women and, 169–73
Relaxing, 176
Reducing. *See* Weight, loss of
Religion, 70, 97–98, 186
    conversion, 44
    marathons and, 98
    nature as catalyst for, 96
    Sunday morning events, 72, 101
Resistance(s) (inhibitions)
    lowering of, 13–14, 24, 75
    overcoming, 150
    See also Psychological barriers
Resistance training, 118
Resonance connection, 140

Resonating with the unconscious, 81–83
Restraints. *See* Resistance(s)
Rhythms, natural, 8, 136
    See also Cycles
Ritual, workout as, 96
Roadrunners Club, 161
Rochester Zen Center, 101
Rogers, Carl, 162
Rolls, head, 30
Rotating femur, 7, 59, 179
Routines, breaking of, 101–2
"Runner's high" (euphoria), 34, 51, 57, 58, 97, 102
    psychotherapy and, 82
Running Home (Spino), 117
Run to Reality (Eischens), 98, 188
Russell, Bertrand, 152
    on creativity, 151

"Safe Harbor," meditation, 107
Safety, of women, 163–64
Saint Luke's Hospital, 34
San Diego Marathon clinic, 70
Schaff, Jack, 124
Schedule, training. *See* Training program
Schizophrenia, 72, 76–77, 183
Schwartz, Steve, 70
"Second wind," 82
Sedentary life-style, 5, 10, 59, 171
    alienation and, 136
    cancer deaths and, 124
    depression and, 35–41
    heart disease and, 61–62
    psychotherapy as, 69
Self, the, 137, 138
Self-analysis, 72
Self-awareness, of women, 176
Self-confidence, 9, 69, 74, 143, 146
    women and, 9, 165–66, 169–73
Self-confrontation, 53–54
Self-consciousness, 23, 80, 89–91, 187

Self-criticism, 7, 52, 53, 91
Self-defense, 163
Self-distraction, 121
Self-healing, meditations for, 125–30
Self-image, 14, 29, 39
Self-mastery, 7, 49
Self-realization (self-actualization, self-affirmation), 3–4, 56, 99
Selye, Hans, 125
Semple, "Jock," 160
Seniors Track Club, 186
Senoi tribe, 93
    "fight or flight" response of, 94–95
Sexuality (sex)
    abstinence, 92–93
    cycles of, 5
    running compared to, 172
Shainberg, David, 103–5
Shake-up, 116
Sheehan, George, 153
Shoes, 31
Shorter, Frank, 66, 68
Shoulder shrugs, 30
Shuffle, 115–18
Simonton, Carl, 124–25
Sit-ups, 29–30
Skin temperature, control of, 123
Sleep, 5
    See also Napping
Sluggishness, 38, 119
Smell, 181, 182
Smith, Ted, 111
Smoking (cigarettes), 25, 26, 51, 52, 62
    heart disease and, 63, 64
Social life, 21
    women and, 169–73
    See also Relationships
Socio-economic status, 104, 141
Socrates, 134
Solitude, 36
Soviet Union, 140
Speed, 144
    endurance and, 28–29

Spino, Dyveke, 107–8, 113
   meditations of, 108–10, 128–
      30
Spino, Michael, 113–14
   Esalen training program of,
      114–19
Spiritual athletes, 111–12
Sprains, 31, 64
Sprinting (sprints), 27, 29
Spontaneity, 10, 11
Stack, "alter," 67
Stamina, 74, 114
Status, socio-economic, 104, 141
Stiffness, 29
Stoic pose, 13, 51
Stomach, 35
   bloating of, 14–17, 21, 32
Stress (strain), 10, 51, 64, 101,
      155
   cardiovascular, 45–47
   cold and, 34
   dream symbolism and, 87
   mental, 7, 36
   "Type A" personalities and,
      62
Strokes, 66
Success
   brain-power increases and,
      153–54
   corporate runners and, 141–42
   image of, 147–49
   James on, 167
   Merrill on, 143
   overthink and, 154–55
   overwork and, 155–56
   running model of, 144–47,
      157
Suggestive learning, 150
Surge, 115–18
Surfaces, 31
Survival, 45, 100
Suzuki, D. T., 105
Swimming, 57
Switzer, Katherine, 53, 160–62,
      164
Synchronicity of body and mind,
      11–14
Synchronous bonding, 6, 138–40

T'ai Chi, 4, 96
Target rate for pulse beats, 26,
      27
Tarahumara Indians, 186
   healing methods of, 130–31
Technique, 22, 144
Teeth, 30
Telepathy, 6, 140, 181
   Freud on, 182
Tempo training, 118
Tendons, 30, 31, 64, 66
Tension(s), 7, 35, 45, 51, 68,
      79, 147, 154
   creativity and, 155–56
   release of, 12–14, 156
Tesquinadas, 186
Testosterone, 33
Therapy. *See* Psychotherapy
Thinking. *See* Thought
Thomas, Lewis, 139
Thompson, Ian, 35
Thompson, William Irwin, 189
Thorazine, 77
Thought (thinking)
   action and, 9–10, 148
   universal forms of, 138, 140
Throat, closing of, 48
Tibetan log meditation, 107
Tibetan monks (Lung Gom Pa),
      106, 113
Timeus (Plato), 10, 133–34
Tiredness (fatigue), 29, 35, 38,
      119, 121
Tissues, connective, 32, 65, 66
Toes, 28
Training program (training
      schedule), 61, 81–82, 144–
      46, 155, 167
   Esalen's, 114–19
   Greist's, 39–40
   during pregnancy, 175–76
   problem-solving and, 152
   for women, 166–68, 175–78
Traits
   genetic, 136, 137
   personality. *See* Personality
Trances, 130, 131

Tranquilizers, 42–43
Transcendental state (transcendence), 6, 56, 102, 135
Triglycerides, 65
Tyler Corporation, 141–42
Tyler Cup race, 142
Type A personalities, 62–64

Ultimate Athlete, The (Leonard), 67, 111, 183
Unconscious, the, 5, 68
    decoding symbols from, 92–95
    healing and, 131
    Paleoanalytic model of, 78–79, 81
    relationships and, 76
    resonating with, 81–83
    stress and, 87
United Nations, 99
Universe
    holographic model of, 135–38
    See also Cosmology
Upper body, 28
Uyeshiba, Morei, 111–12

Van Aaken, Ernst, 159
Verbal ability, 11–12
Vertical push-ups, 30
Visceral learning, 180–85
Visual perception. *See* Perception changes
Visualization(s) (mental imagery), 119–22
    cancer patients and, 124–25
    physiological control and, 124
    of success, 148
Vitamins, 32

Waist, 28
Warm-ups, 29–30, 64
    for pregnant women, 176
Weight, losing, 14, 63, 65, 71, 99
Weight problems, 15–17, 26
Westerbeke Ranch, 109
Wheelock, John, 105
Will, the
    collective, 139
    as muscle, 145–46
"Witness self," 121
Women, 7
    androgyny and, 158, 164–66
    body-mind synchronicity and, 14–25
    clothes for, 31
    in competition with men, 167–69
    discrimination against, 158–61
    endurance of, 159–60
    in marathons, 168–69
    motivation of, 165
    over forty, 176–78
    physical pleasure and, 172–73
    pregnant, 173–76
    psychological barriers of, 161–64
    safety of, 163–64
    self-confidence and, 9, 165–66, 169–73
Work (careers, jobs), 29, 38
    changes in, 72–73
    energy for, 69–70
Workouts. *See* Training program

Yeast infection, 31
Yogis, 113

Zen-like states or experiences, 4, 97, 101–3